Arnold White

The Problems of a Great City

Arnold White

The Problems of a Great City

ISBN/EAN: 9783744790741

Printed in Europe, USA, Canada, Australia, Japan

Cover: Foto ©Suzi / pixelio.de

More available books at **www.hansebooks.com**

See Page 138. On retention of dead bodies in living rooms.

THE PROBLEMS OF A GREAT CITY

BY

ARNOLD WHITE

LONDON
REMINGTON & CO PUBLISHERS
HENRIETTA STREET COVENT GARDEN

1886
[*All Rights Reserved*]

I INSCRIBE ALL THAT
IS GOOD IN THIS BOOK TO
ONE WHO BY HER LIFE AND EXAMPLE HAS
ADDED WISDOM TO GENEROSITY, AND WHOSE ONLY FEAR
IS THE DISCOVERY BY THE PUBLIC OF GREAT
DEEDS DONE IN SECRET AND NOT
FOR FAME.

CONTENTS.

CHAP.		PAGE
	PREFACE.	
I.	The Whited Wall	1
II.	The National Debt	11
III.	Sterilization of the Unfit...	27
IV.	Emigration	64
V.	Colonization	116
VI.	Overcrowding	130
VII.	Adulteration	154
VIII.	Drink	164
IX.	Socialism...	179
X.	The Poor Man's Budget...	208
XI.	The Unemployed	223
XII.	Charities ...	245
	CONCLUSION.	259

PREFACE.

WHOEVER would grapple with the Problems of a Great City, must bear the burden of a heavy heart. The nature of the task, the failure of bygone efforts, the apathy of the comfortable classes, discourage fresh attempts to set forth remedies for evils visible to all. Any contribution, however, towards the settlement of the Social question, if prepared thoughtfully and with labour, and presented with a humble sense of inherent deficiencies, may perhaps be accepted as an instalment of the solution Society itself alone can apply.

CHAPTER I.

THE WHITED WALL.

INHABITANTS of the British Islands are prone to plume themselves on the spectacle they present to gods and men. It is, nevertheless, a question whether the texture of British civilization is sufficiently tough to stand examination; or whether the organization of society will compare with the sociology of certain among the Himalayan tribes, or with the Basuto, Zulu, or Amatonga nations, upon whose conversion we are annually wont to lay out a portion of our savings. Such is the falling off from the ideal set forth in the Sermon on the Mount, that our thirty-eight millions of nominal Christians are not only no better, but, in certain characteristics, are distinctly inferior to a like number of Buddhists or Mahommedans. Drunkenness and pauperism, organized villainy, secret crimes, adulteration, fraud and cruelty in England are perpetrated with a lustiness and resolve foreign to the Asiatic mind. It is true that certain forms of vice are more perfectly developed in Asia than in England. But it is no less true that Eastern society is free from the taint of organized hypocrisy which, in our own case, drugs the national conscience, if it do not impose on the public opinion of the rest of mankind.

In the books of the three Pitakas a code of ethics is laid down which finds no followers in practice. The ideal is unattainable. The motive for sacrifice is of phantom-fabric. It exists only in theory.

The beatitudes of Gautama are not well known, and they are less followed.

> Not to serve the foolish,
> But to serve the wise;
> To honour those worthy of honour:
>   This is the greatest blessing.

To dwell in a pleasant land,
Good works done in a former birth,
Right desires in the heart:
    This is the greatest blessing.

Much insight and education,
Self-control and pleasant speech,
And whatever word be well spoken:
    This is the greatest blessing.

To support father and mother,
To cherish wife and child,
To follow a peaceful calling:
    This is the greatest blessing,

To bestow alms and live righteously,
To give help to kindred,
Deeds which cannot be blamed:
    These are the greatest blessing.

To abhor, and cease from sin,
Abstinence from strong drink,
Not to be weary in well doing,
    These are the greatest blessing.

Reverence and lowliness,
Contentment and gratitude,
The hearing of the Law at due seasons,
    This is the greatest blessing.

To be long-suffering and meek,
To associate with the tranquil
Religious talk at due seasons,
    This is the greatest blessing.

> Self-restraint and purity,
> The knowledge of the Noble Truths,
> The realization of Nirvana,
> > This is the greatest blessing.
>
> Beneath the stroke of life's changes,
> The mind that shaketh not,
> Without grief or passion, and secure,
> > This is the greatest blessing.
>
> On every side are invincible,
> They who do acts like these,
> On every side they walk in safety,
> > And theirs is the greatest blessing.

As a necessary result of the contrast between profession and practice it is found that when the conventional Buddhist encounters reverses, or confronts a serious crisis in his life, he abandons the philosophy of Gautama, and betakes himself, under the storm of necessity, to the establishment of relations with the powers of evil.

Not otherwise is the method of the conventional Christian of the West. The lives and characters of the main body of those who assert, and of those who professionally explain the teachings of the Sermon on the Mount, are a strange study to an orthodox Moslem or pious Hindoo. With an assured income, proceeding from safe investments returning four and a quarter per cent., it is difficult for a prosperous Christian to be poor in spirit. He is neither reviled nor persecuted. So far from any man saying all manner of evil against him for Christ's sake, the reputation of "goodness" carries with it a professional advantage. To be accounted as an "earnest" man; to occupy a seat on the Board of a Foreign Missionary Society; to hold views on the sanctity of the Sabbath; to be the author of a luscious hymn, are proved methods of mundane advancement. To agree with his adversary quickly, is an archaic form of stating the advantages of compromise.

The struggling trader finds it a harder matter to maintain the ideal of the Mount. Discounts and drawbacks, the relation of samples to deliveries, the statements of advertisements, the representations of commercial travellers, and the exigencies of competition, and of the adulteration which Mr. Bright holds to be one of the forms of competition, place him in a position of strained relations with the Socialism of his Teacher.

Difficulties, all but insuperable to rich men,

are overcome with no greater ease by those in humbler station. As the conscience becomes tender and the convictions strong, the work of common life trenches on the region that is Tabu. If A surrenders his brewery and a fortune for conscience' sake, because he will not face the responsibility of the death and degradation awaiting some, at all events, of the clients of the family tap, how can B, the conscientious vatman, retain his employment? He knows that the beer which he assists to brew, judiciously blended with salt and *indicus cocculus* by needy middle-men, will bemuse and degrade a certain number of his brothers and sisters in blood.

Cutting off the right hand, and mutilating the eyesight, would now subject the convert to the charge of fanaticism, if not to seclusion in an establishment for the insane. To refrain from doing our alms before men would deprive example of half its force, besides impairing the security of many a seat in Parliament. To abandon the defence of private rights would give to Mr. Hyndman, and to men like the late Mr. Peace, too favourable a field for the exercise of their abilities. Strict obedience to the command, "Take no thought what ye shall eat," would subject many an honoured saint to claret a shade too warm. Is he to kill the "old man" until he is indifferent to the catastrophe of an overdressed canvas-back duck? Who among the comfortable classes can feel that the triumph of mind and spirit over body and matter is such that he cares not whether his wine be Cape claret or Clos Vongeout: whether he smokes shag tobacco or Partagas Imperiales; or, if a woman, whether she has that sense of being perfectly well dressed—a sense which, as the French cynic tells us, confers a sense of peace religion itself is powerless to bestow—or whether she is a frump?

Nonconformist objections restrict the enjoyment to be obtained from rioting in religious statistics. It is revealed, however, by the faithful Whitaker, that the forms of faith followed in the British Islands number at least one hundred and ninety-one. Among them they have founded societies to assuage every evil, and to combat every error. Lost dogs and lost women, other folks' servants, equatorial Africans, and English Jews, tons of tracts, and bewildered emigrants, engage the confused energies of thousands of first-class hearts and fourth-class heads. From time to time society is stirred by a movement of wider influence; and, as in the case of General Booth's enterprise, receives the blessings and the anathemas which are equally effectual in conferring the desired notoriety and in obtaining the necessary cash. As the upper classes lounge and travel, dress, bet, shoot, race and struggle through the miasmatic lowlands of *ennui* with more or less success, without being driven to the practice of an active faith, the middle and lower classes find in the vocabulary and emotion of religion cheap and effectual antidotes to the dreary monotony of their unlovely lives. Or, as a sage puts it, "the lower classes care as little for the dogmas of religion as the upper classes care for its practice." They are palsied eyes, however, that cannot discover here and there on the prairie of convention, flower-souls reflecting the glory of the blue sky in all its beauty and simplicity, adorned with the greatness of unselfish life, because they live to abandon the aim and end of personal ease and personal fame. Such a one was Gordon. His legacy to the English people is not fully understood, because the legatees can enjoy it only by a personal administration of the trust.

Since the Sermon on the Mount has been sub-edited by English society and their teachers in accordance with the requirements of a high standard of comfort, the luxury of the few confronts the misery of millions with a sharpness of contrast hitherto achieved by no nation since the story of mankind was first written. Religion has become a thing of words and buildings. Religion endowed so that the carriage of the Cross is ofttimes the means to win high place and high comfort, has converted the Narrow Way into a path to the House of Lords as well as to the Place of a Skull. Were Christ the Teacher to return to London, how long would He remain aloof from an attack on the problems of a great City? Responsibility exists, and cannot be explained away. On our rulers and on our teachers the heavy burden lies; but there are few whose rest is troubled by the thought of the things undone that ought to be done, or by the shame that would drive away all sleep from their eyes if those eyes could see and understand the remediable wrongs inflicted on a stricken and a feeble folk.

CHAPTER II.

THE NATIONAL DEBT.

ORACLES, who have never lacked a cutlet, tell us that the conditions of industrial life in England contrast favourably with those prevailing in countries where the standard of comfort is lower. Nevertheless, the social question in England is shrouded in greater darkness than the social questions of Imperial Germany or Republican France. Nowhere in Berlin or in Paris can be found the surging crowd of passionate seekers for work, who fight as wild beasts at the London Dock Gates on winter mornings with monotony of want. It is true that here and there, as at Liège, Décazeville, or Antwerp, there is an eruption of the Continental proletariat into aimless fury against their rulers. Great Britain has a rough average of 800,000 paupers entertained by the State, and probably half a million more supported from the resources of charity. No comparison, therefore, can be instituted between the English and Continental social questions without an allowance for the fact that, however appalling the mass of our national misery may be, provision has already been made for at least a million and a quarter of our social failures, who, but for the premium of insurance known as the Poor Law, would anticipate the coming struggle between the Haves and the Have-nots by several years. Great as was the sum of poverty and degradation inherited by this generation from that which preceded it, we are making no sensible reductions of this debt to humanity, and are in a fair way to hand down to the next generation greater embarrassment, with more efficient machinery for the manufacture of larger masses of human degradation. Such is the financial chastity of the present school of statesmen, that the maintenance of the national money debt at its present figure is regarded with abhorrence, and the suspension of the Sinking fund is resorted to only under the menace of national calamity. The money debt is now £740,330,654, or less than £20 per head. In 1815 it was £45 per head. While, therefore, liability for past expenditure has relatively diminished, responsibility for the submerged stratum of our fellow-subjects has increased to almost unmanageable dimensions. In London alone there is a Norwich full of prostitutes; a Huntingdon full of known criminals; two Nottinghams full of folk without homes; for whom famine is ever on the horizon, and deficiency of food always in the foreground. As the rich grow richer the poor get poorer. Between Dives and Lazarus the great gulf fixed becomes deeper, wider, and blacker month by month and year by year. Imagination is needed to believe that once upon a time the Thames flowed clear at the Tower, or that our country was ever known as Merry England. Night by night, and day by day, rise through the canopy of smoke the lamentations of those who rue the day they were born. I have seen men throw themselves on the granite setts of the street, praying for death to end the hopeless misery of want of food and want of work. I have heard the wailing of hungry children, locked foodless into a bare insanitary room, while the mother, stung to exertion by maternal instinct all too soon after recent child-birth, seeks, like a beast of prey, for wherewithal to stay the famine of her young ones. I have watched unseen, strong men who had served their Queen, gaunt with want, gaze wistfully from the bridge parapet at the dark waters of the Thames, longing to end troubles thrust upon them by the way of the world. From the cheap lodging-houses, from the railway arches, from the crowded streets, rises an ever-increasing volume of inarticulate and unquenchable misery. Compared with the nomadic tribes of tropic countries, where the curse of civilization is unknown, the nomads of London are but miserable savages. Capable of greater suffering, they are condemned to acuter pain. Hypocrisy, when crime fails, as a last resort may yield a crust. Mission rooms, covered with a rash of texts—Chaldee to the hungry and broken man—are open to the vagrant and the " dosser." But it cannot be denied that, notwithstanding the combined efforts of all the churches and the machinery of all the societies, no real advance is being made in the process of killing out the prolific powers of evil. Statistics published by an optimistic Home Secretary may satisfy those who wish to blunt their sense of personal responsibility, that the curves of official pauperism and of crime are ever sinking in comparison with the numbers of the population.

The curve of misery is not included in official returns. It is not to be obtained either at the Local Government Board or at the Home Office. Ministers are not always to blame. They, poor souls, are but pith figures, dancing only when the electricity of public opinion energizes the cellulose of their puppet systems. When the current is at rest, their strength is to sit still, and thus the fatal moment of collision between the classes and the masses approaches with astronomical certainty.

As many causes have led to the existence of the social question, it is idle to look for one sovereign cure and one alone. Panaceas do not exist to transmute the corrosion of national life into a healing process. As the causes are various, the remedies are many; and none is to be despised because it contributes but little to the solution of the problem. No man has hitherto attempted to deal with the social question as a whole. Many have concentrated energy on a stray symptom of the disease, and look for restored health when the general adoption of their own specific is an accomplished fact. Temperance people hold drink to be the cause of distress, though it is laid down by others that distress is the cause of the drink. Reckless and improvident marriages are considered by Malthusians to be at the root of our social trouble. Liberation of labour and the overthrow of the present economical system is believed by the advertised followers of Marx and Lassalle to be the right way to get behind the north wind in the struggle for existence. Those who have emerged from the competitive struggle with the spoils of war are justifiably content with the system of *laissez-faire*. " The poor in the lump is bad" is the standpoint of many besides the Northern Farmer. Free trade and unfettered liberty for the play of economic laws is the gospel of the "fat and greasy citizen;" and any effort to lay impious hands on the ark of free contract is the unpardonable sin. Freedom! Liberty! Freedom to starve; liberty to go to the devil. If Bismarck Cromwellizes the frontiers of the Fatherland, and thousands of Polish and German Jews fly to Whitechapel, Saint George's-in-the-East, Clerkenwell, and Bethnal Green, the master sweating-tailors are free to extort harder work for lower wage from their women and girl workers of English blood on account of the competition of foreign cheap labour; and the girl-wives and daughters are free to hawk their persons in the streets of our English city to fill up the chasm caused by the operation of the law of unrestricted competition. Reflection alone is needed to show that the death struggle of carnivorous animals, and the logical consequence of unrestricted freedom of contract, are convertible terms. The following is a statement from authoritative sources, expressed in official language :—

"Female labour is wretchedly paid. In shirt-making (for export) and similar employment a woman gets about ninepence to a shilling for a day's work of sixteen hours. There are hundreds of women who work for three-farthings an hour and find their own needles and cotton. The prices include: Shirts, three-farthings each; flannel drawers for Chelsea pensioners, one shilling and threepence a dozen; soldiers' leggings, two shillings a dozen; and lawn-tennis aprons, elaborately frilled, fivepence-halfpenny a dozen to the 'sweater,' the actual worker getting much less. In such kinds of women's work, however, the whole profit does not, as is supposed, go to the 'sweater,' but finds its way in great measure into the pockets of the middle-men and retail dealers. The public, too, have often in some degree the benefit of these starvation wages."

The following details of fifty men employed by sweating tailors were obtained in reply to questions addressed to the men themselves:—

QUESTIONS.

Age (years)?—2 at 16; 1 at 18; 3 at 19; 2 at 21; 5 at 22; 2 at 24; 5 at 25; 2 at 26; 3 at 27; 3 at 28; 3

at 30 and 31; 1 at 34; 3 at 35; 3 at 36; 1 at 37; 1 at 39; 3 at 40; 1 at 45; 1 at 51; 2 at 56.

Single or married?—40 married; 10 single.

If married how many children?—4 with none; 9 with 1; 5 with 2; 7 with 3; 6 with 4; 3 with 5; 5 with 6.

Wages of good machinists per day?—6 at 6s.; 2 at 6s. 6d.; 10 at 7s.; 3 at 6s. 8d.; 17 at 7s. 6d.; 8 at 8s.; 1 at 8s. 6d. 1 at 1s. 1d. each coat; 1 at 1s. 6d. each coat; 1 at 4d. per waistcoat.

Wages of plain machinists per day?—1 at 1s.; 2 at 2s.; 1 at 2s. 6d.; 8 at 3s.; 4 at 3s. 6d.; 1 at 3s. 8d.; 1 at 3s. 9d.; 15 at 4s.; 1 at 4s. 6d.; 7 at 5s.; 3 at 5s. 6d.; 2 at 6s.; 3 at 6s. 8d.

How many girls at work, and wages per day?—1 at 10d.; 1 at 1s. 2d.; 1 at 1s. 3d.; 4 at 1s. 6d.; 5 at 1s. 8d.; 8 at 2s.; 17 at 2s. 6d.; 22 at 3s.; 1 at 3s. 3d.; 6 at 3s. 6d.; 2 at 3s. 8d.; 6 at 4s.; 1 at 4s. 6d.; 2 at 4s. 8d.; 7 at 5s.

Is there a coke fire in same workshop?—46 cases coke fire; 4 cases gas stove.

How many gaslights?—In 2 cases, 3; in 6 cases, 4; in 11 cases, 5; in 8 cases, 6; in 11 cases, 7; in 3 cases, 8; in 2 cases, 9; in 2 cases, 12; in 2 cases, 15; in 1 case, one lamp; in one case, 5; in 1 case paraffin.

How many water closets?—In 47 cases 1, two being described as "very dirty."

What hours do the men work per day?—In 2 cases 10; in 6 cases, 13; in 11 cases, 14; in 1 case, $14\frac{1}{2}$; in 16 cases, 15; in 7 cases, 16; in 2 cases, 17; in 3 cases, 18; in 1 case, 19; in 1 case, 20.

What hours do the girls work per day?—In 1 case $10\frac{1}{2}$; in 3 cases, 11; in 17 cases, 12; in 3 cases, $12\frac{1}{2}$; in 14 cases, 13; in 10 cases, 14; in 2 cases, work in kitchen after 11 and 12 respectively; in one case 12 hours, and paid for ¾ day; in 2 cases, 12 hours, paid for 11; in 1 case till 10 Thursday; in 1 case till 11; in 1 case 15 hours; in 1 case 14 hours Thursday. In 1 case, sometimes in kitchen after 11.

How often does Inspector visit workshop?—In 9 cases, "Very seldom;" in 2 cases, "Very often;" in 4 cases, "Once;" in 3 cases, "Once in three months;" in 2 cases, "Twice in two years;" in 19 cases, "Never;" in 1 case, "Once in 6 months;" in 3 cases, "Been twice." (In 3 cases fines imposed, one of these paying two penalties.)

What time do men leave work Thursday night?—In 3 cases at 10; in 1 case at 10.30; in 3 cases at 11; in 2 cases at 11.30; in 17 cases at 12; in 2 cases at 12.30; in 8 cases at 1; in 4 cases at 2; in 1 case at 2.30; in 1 case at 3; in 1 case at 4. In 2 cases, "sometimes all night;" in 1 case, "as usual;" in 1 case, "don't leave shop."

What time do they come on Friday morning?—In 1 case at 4; in 9 cases at 5; in 20 cases at 6; in 3 cases at 6.30; in 10 cases at 7; in 2 cases at 8; in 1 case at 10; in 1 case no work Friday.

Do they have an hour for dinner on Friday?—In 45 cases, "No;" in 5 cases not stated either way; 1 case out of these says "No, even middle of week."

Are your wages reduced in the slack time?—In 2 cases, 6d.; in 3 cases, 1s.; in 1 case, 2s.; in 2 cases, takes off quarter day; in 22 cases, "No;" in 17 cases, "Yes;" in one case discharges men.

How long have you to work for half-day?—In 11 cases, 7 hours; in 6 cases, 7½ hours; in 20 cases, 8 hours; in 3 cases, 8½ hours; in 9 cases, 9 hours; in 1 case, "off at 12."

How many hours for quarter-day?—In 5 cases, 3½ hours;

in 2 cases, 4¼ hours; in 22 cases, 4 hours; in 7 cases, 4½ hours; in 12 cases, 5 hours; in 1 case, 6 hours; in 1 case, 7 hours.

The following are some of the remarks appended to the questions by the men themselves :—

If there are two hours' work we must oblige them for nothing — Drives us like slaves, or as if we were dogs, and calls us foul names, and swears and curses all day—Too many to put down—Sometimes work all night, and get paid for quarter of a day—Not paid in full for time worked—Sometimes, if I work four and a half days, get paid for three and three-quarters—Have to work any time when wanted, and not paid—Drives us like dogs—Treated very bad—Very badly treated; children play in the workshop—If I complain of the many hours, he says, " Go home, you are only fit for cat's meat;" and sends the apprentice to find him another horse—The workshop is in a dilapidated condition, and not fit for a wild beast to be in it; the ceiling falling through day by day, and raining in—When he expects the Inspector, he puts the poor girls in his bedroom or kitchen, and many a Thursday night the poor girls don't go home to sleep—The master ought to be buried, as he is very bad—The apprentice has to be left after other girls are gone—I have cruel treatment, and he always tries to take as much off wages as possible; he tries his utmost—He is a bad man—as good as the lot—very cruel, and thinks nothing of a workman, calls them his horses—Paid Sunday instead of when leaving off—A very spiteful man—Employers have decided to give their men piece-work, which is greatly to the disadvantage of the *employé*, reduces wages to nothing—Very bad man, not worth serving—Very bad master—We work all the week and he pays us three times, and he goes about the workshop grumbling that we work too short hours; he says that we got to work from six to twelve at night—The employer don't care to get up early, and tries to detain you as long as possible in the evening—Very insulting—Never work on Friday, but finish and don't get paid for it—He is very insulting.

A cabinet-maker working by the piece, who must sell the fruit of his week's work or starve, is free only in one sense. The other party to the contract is free in another. Englishmen are governed by phrases. The most beneficent institution, were it entitled " Star Chamber," would stand no chance of winning the public confidence. " Home Rule " has destroyed the Liberal party; " Local Self-Government " is conceded by all parties alike. So with " freedom " and " slavery." Oriental London enjoys the advantages of the worst and most squalid forms of slavery under the name of freedom, and therefore there is nothing incongruous when a million and a quarter of pounds sterling are annually despatched for the souls of fat heathen in more favoured corners of the earth's surface, or in the complacency with which we look back on the liberation of the West Indian slaves.

Misery and despair, loathing of the curse of life, mocked with the vocabulary of religion, groanings that cannot be uttered, an ever-growing torrent of children poured into an environment of wretchedness and vice, are some of the chemicals seething in the caldron of civilization. Abroad we have done no better. Tribes chaste and temperate are decimated by loathsome diseases, and ruined by raw spirits proffered by the hand that does not hold the Bible.

Many a valiant soul fights gallantly to stem the tide of woe and want. But their efforts, if not fruitless, make no permanent and palpable impress on the mass of wrong to be cleared away. Ever increasing at compound interest, the volume of our national debt grows with rapid strides, and even now the mutterings of subterranean fires can be heard by those who have ears to ear and who are not muffled in comfort. Every winter a bitter cry is raised by permanent distress. Fleeting notice is attracted, and twopence-halfpenny apiece for all in trouble is raised by the influence of a Mansion House Committee and the destruction of a few Piccadilly windows. Then the leaf buds burst, and Ascot, Henley, strawberries, and Strauss's band chase the ugly memories of the winter through the Ivory Gate.

What is to be done in order to liquidate the National Debt? The right course to pursue may be doubtful, but it is clear that this is no time to stand in the ancient ways. The present system of the churches after a course of evangelical teaching extending over one hundred and fifty years has failed beyond hope of redemption. Philanthropy is a paid profession supporting swarms of administrators. The struggle for existence between benevolent societies is as bitter as the strife between the various forms of the Christian faith, or between members of the same Cabinet. Disease has corroded the texture of civilization, and such an analysis as was never bestowed upon it is needed before prescriptions can be prepared and exhibited to the suffering nation with any hope of success. Diagnosis of the disease is not impossible. The evil is broadly divisible into two parts—the remediable and that which is essentially incapable of cure. The remediable portion is again to be divided into (1) That which can be attacked and dealt with by society at large forthwith, and (2) That which requires the process of time for the development of healing measures. In other words, the work for this generation is one part, and work for the next generation is the second portion of the task. Then again, the remedies applicable by society, either legislative or otherwise, are precedent to the efforts of those on whose behalf society bestirs itself. The work as a whole is a process and not a stroke. It cannot be carried out by legislation alone. Law is nothing more than the floating opinion of the majority of the people, crystallized in the form of an Act of Parliament. Law that is in advance of or behind the convictions of the majority is inoperative. The Act of Charles II. on Sunday Trading, and the Contagious Diseases Acts lately repealed, are instances of each contingency.

That which is required, therefore, is the

creation of wholesome public opinion in regard to specific evils needing prompt and drastic treatment, and the excitement of such a sense of universal individual responsibility that it can neither be alienated nor evaded. We need the Conscription for social affairs. The party of Social Reform is at present in agreement about nothing, although most people have a general conviction that a great deal requires to be done, with a leaning towards drugs from their own pharmacopœia. Convention, and its cousin Decorum, combine with the safe formalities of a Christianity ignorant of its Founder, to prevent discussion or inquiry into some of the root causes of the evil. The art of embellishing the outside of the platter is incapable of further development. We live in the golden age of whited walls. Any poor wight, therefore, who is resolute in stripping horror of its clothing may lay to his account the certain enmity of most of the clergy and all the paid philanthropists who batten on the process of whiting the wall with a dainty brush of camels' hair.

CHAPTER III.

STERILIZATION OF THE UNFIT.

PROBLEMS unsolved, and prayers ungranted abound. No problem is more perplexing than the steady advance of democratic power, while the physical and mental strength and health of a large fraction of the democracy are undermined by the conditions of their lives. Democratic Government means the inclusion of those who are ignorant of the laws of hereditary transmission, who are least prepared to lay down present ease for future good, and who are least accustomed to resist the impulse of passion or the suggestions of desire. Democratic Government means the inclusion of those who are the results of immature, and often of pauper, marriages. Medical science mitigates suffering, but preserves the diseased. Maladies arising from profligacy are controlled and half cured. Natural penalties of excess are remitted by medical science. Sanitary precautions, poor laws, vaccination, hospitals, charity, save from death and preserve to marry and to vote, thousands of those who must lead dismal and imperfect lives, and who, but for the meddling of science, would have died. Thus, the destinies of England depend on the issue of a struggle between moral and mental enlightenment and mental and physical deterioration. Tainted constitutions, brains charged with subtle mischief, and languishing or extinct morality, transmit a terrible inheritance of evil to the next generation, there to taint once more a whole community. And those who multiply as ephemera are the squalid inhabitants of hovels subsisting on degraded and adulterated foods; and acquiring their joys from the gratification of lust, and the absorption in excess of drugged and poisonous forms of alcohol. We thus have a practical example of the fact that the tendency of the higher civilization is to multiply from the lower and not from the higher specimens of the race. A higher average of life has been bought at the price of a lower average of health. In low and miserable neighbourhoods the amount of labour lost in the year, not by illness, but by sheer exhaustion and inability to do the work, amounts, on the lowest average, to twenty days in the year.*

The species is being propagated and continued increasingly, though not of course exclusively, from the idle, unthrifty, undersized, and unfit. As luxury and success corrupt the West End, the East is corrupted by want and failure. As in the West there are those who, born to wealth, revelling in wealth, are destitute of the qualities by which wealth is won, or its possession made a blessing to the community : so in the East, those born to poverty, wallowing in misery, are, many of them, devoid of the qualities by which life is sustained in dignity, if not in comfort, and perpetuated by means of a healthy and capable progeny. Comfort-worship in the West leads to extra-

* Blue Book, C. 4402-28. See also the Report of the Royal Commission on the Housing of the Poor.

vagant prudence. Comfort-worship in the East leads to despair and its consequences. It is thus that the very rich and the very poor marry as early as they please—the motive to abstain is absent from either class. The trustworthy, energetic element of the population—those who long to rise and do not choose to sink—abstain from marriage. Favourites of fortune and the desperate classes are those who most freely undertake the responsibilities of parentage, and from whom the population is replenished.

If it be monstrous that the weak should be destroyed by the strong, how much more repugnant it is to instinct and to reason that the strong and capable should be overwhelmed by the feeble, ailing, and unfit?

To prevent such a catastrophe it is needful that society should recognize as essential —

1. That, preceding the production of children, should be the power or the prospect of maintaining them.

2. That the propagation of diseased or infected constitutions shall be condemned, or even regarded as criminal. Such diseases as scrofula, consumption, and syphilis are amen-

able to the conditions under which leprosy and plague have become extinct diseases in England and in America. A moderate expansion of this idea would lead to the extermination of the unfit as a class.

3. That idleness and dissipation are discreditable in all classes.

As our tenderness to suffering is accompanied by a gentleness towards wrong, it is impossible to grapple with the suffering caused by wrong without shocking the gentleness of society.

One Doubleday, forty years ago, hit on a theory which has since received the sanction of better known men. The lower down in the scale of creation, and the worse fed, the greater the fertility, was the substance of his idea. The whale brings forth but one or two at a birth. Animalculæ forming the staple diet of the whale provide for posterity millions of their kind. Elephants and herrings, the dwellers in Grosvenor Square and in Collier's Rents, Borough, are examples testifying to the accuracy of observations made by the late Mr. Doubleday. It is regrettable that the relative fecundity of the comfortable and the uncomfortable classes is not established beyond cavil or dispute, by the process of official investigation; but sufficient *data* exist to place the fundamental correctness of the theory beyond reasonable attack. Anyone who is sufficiently interested in the inductive method to make an investigation for himself can do no better than to compare a list of his married friends and their children with a like number of families who are actually engaged in the struggle for existence east of Aldgate Church. The results obtained will be surprising to those who are content to believe that the population of England is increasing on safe lines. The unemployed and unfit classes marry early and often. Prudence in their connubial arrangements is unknown, as we shall see hereafter. The annual increase in the population proceeds mainly from the classes who add no strength to the nation. In the process of filling their quivers, the folk whose normal lot is to be within half-a-crown of starvation are countenanced by many of the clergy of all denominations; and, excepting the Roman Catholic Church, they add to their clerical precepts the force of a vigorous example. To be fruitful and multiply in London involves a suppressed injunction to starve, or live on other people. In the lowest class of all marriage is all but unknown. Vicious celibacy is the rule, and liberal contributions to the illegitimacy rate are supplied from the nomadic tribes infesting the darker haunts of London.

In England marriage is fixed at the age of puberty, as defined in the Roman Law—viz., fourteen for males and twelve for females. The absence of the consent of parents or guardians does not invalidate a marriage.

The Code Napoléon (Arts. 144-226) prescribes the ages of eighteen for the man and fifteen for the woman. A son under twenty-five and a daughter under twenty-one cannot marry without the consent of the father and mother, or of the father only if they disagree, or of the survivor if one be dead.

Precocious marriage in the East End is prevalent to an extent inconceivable to the prudent mind of the West, and is followed by disunion, separation, adultery, and recourse to charity or the rates. It is recorded by the Rev. J. W. Horsley that of 176 cases of premature marriage which came under his notice in Clerkenwell Prison, in one case the husband had been fourteen years of age when he abandoned the irresponsible position of bachelor life. This young gentleman was subsequently apprehended for trigamy when thirty-four. In eleven cases the wife was fourteen years old. In two cases the husband, and in twelve the wife, was fifteen. In twelve cases the husband, in forty-six the wife, and in three cases both were sixteen. Twenty-seven husbands and forty-eight wives were seventeen when they began housekeeping, and in thirteen cases both of the happy pair boasted of that age. Alcoholic infanticide is the usual consequence of this class of union, though they are complacently included in that high marriage rate which is held out as one of the prouder features of English social life. The law gives no power either to the clergy or to registrars to delay such unnatural alliances, when the consent of parents or guardians is not withheld. Half a hundred banns of marriage are gabbled over on a Sunday morning in some East End churches, and the clergy not unnaturally feel that the quantity of marriages absolves them from responsibility. Wild weather comes too soon to these silly boys and girls, but the evil inflicted on society by their reckless incontinence is greater still. True, we must face a somewhat increased illegitimacy rate, were these marriages prevented by law, but if we thrust aside the phrase, and look into the essence of the thing, it is beyond dispute that a small increase of illegitimacy is a lesser evil than a large though legalised production of thieves and prostitutes.

In the East End every boy of fourteen or fifteen keeps company with his "bit of frock." At seventeen or eighteen marriage is contemplated, and at nineteen or twenty it is often, if not generally, perpetrated. Marriage! The sanction of the Church of England and of the high and mighty court of Parliament is accorded to these loathsome unions; and these august bodies are therefore accessory to the manufacture of the diseased and incapable children who bubble out of the ground for torment in this world if not in the next.

East End marriages are often "solemnized"

hurriedly on Sunday mornings by tired curates in empty churches. At the "Red Church" the fee is sevenpence. This church is popularly distinguished by a title which cannot be reproduced here. The following statement of the methods in which this tie is contracted was published by the Rev. Charles L. Marson, a competent witness, and the facts recorded therein have not been contradicted by the responsible clergy :—

"The church door was securely barred, and ingress was with difficulty effected.

"This was a double precaution : to prevent more grog being brought into the church, and to prevent the escape of semi-intoxicated bridegrooms. Inside the church was a noisy, indecorous crowd. Doubtful jokes were being bandied about, which grew coarser and coarser as time went on. Hats were freely worn, and drink bottles were passed to and fro, and handed across the aisles. Every now and then a prayer book or other missile was playfully thrown by one of the crowd.

"After a long interval, during which the legal business was being transacted, the ceremony began, and my informant gradually worked his way up to the west end. The method pursued was to call the Christian names of the men together, and all the Christian names of the women, and insert the words 'in each case.'

"Thus the forty couples were united in holy matrimony.

"One man was so recalcitrant, he had to be led three times, drunk as he was, up to the altar; when my informant protested against the indecency of allowing the ceremony in his case to proceed, but was told that the drunken bridegroom was already legally married. The bag was then handed round for the freewill offerings, and amid a shower of the coarsest jokes freely shouted after them, the newly-married went out of the church.

"Outside, the foulest and most indecent jests met them, and pantomimic acting of the worst kind; and thus ended the ceremony which celebrated their entrance into the mystical union of marriage.

"My own experience, and that of several others, bears out this account in the minutest particulars, and I have more than once followed the bride and bridegroom to the nearest pothouse. One man told me he was married at the age of eighteen in the Red Church, and his 'party boozed until tea-time,' which he thought was the usual custom 'immediately afterwards.' Several of the bridegrooms, while still in church, declared, with an oath, that they were off for beer, and they called loudly upon their friends to join them.

"No wonder that there is a current popular belief that 'marriage at the Red Church brings ill-luck with it.' Thus lightly undertaken, one expects next to hear of these marriages at the House, and the Relieving Officers report that the majority of married women admitted to the workhouse for their first confinement were married at the Red Church.

"What work is built upon the basis of these marriages? Seemingly none. A curious person who wandered into the Red Church upon the first Sunday of the month saw a curious sight. One young lady, two clergy, and an organist, the organ-blower, and two infirm old ladies formed the congregation. About the end of the Litany old women began to drop in by twos and threes, until there were twenty-two of them in all. One even brought an epileptic husband with her. The last woman came in, and asked the stranger 'how long the old gentleman' (the preacher) 'had been up there.' In turn he asked her how there was such a large congregation, and was told carelessly, 'They come for the coals—that's all.' 'How much coal do you get for coming?' 'Only 14—still it's worth coming for.' Thus the opportunity of knitting together into a congregation the people who come into the church is entirely lost, and the Red Church does hardly anything else than harm.

"The East London marriages are a most depressing subject for contemplation. They neither hallow life, nor are legally punctilious as a general rule. They do not tend in the least degree to deepen the sanctity of the marriage tie, to give the lie to a blasphemous political economy, to inculcate self-restraint and awe. They are performed with yawning, hurry, and neglect, sometimes with every antithesis to sanctity, and can only be remembered as dry legal facts, which would be more efficiently chronicled under the civil code. We should not readily hear the last of a drinking bout performed with sacramental cups; but this would be quite a light form of irreligion to that which weekly goes on in our churches, where the sacrament of marriage is profaned and degraded until it is drained dry of all holy ghostliness, and presents nothing but the foul dregs of impurity, carelessness, and irreligious animalism."

The opinion of an able and experienced clergyman, who writes under the *nom-de-plume* of "Peter the Hermit," and who has done a great and noble work for many years, is as follows:—

"One thing I have given up all hope of, and that is, influencing boys or girls see to the folly of premature engagements and unions. These have grown too much the practice of the world they live in. Everyone in their class marries early, and a large proportion prematurely— that is, while still in their teens. I have talked for hours, days, weeks, months, nay years, to the most sensible, and most under my influence in other respects, and tried to dissuade them; but all in vain. They listen and laugh, and think I am looking at the world through spectacles of my own. 'Oh, no,' they say, 'we will wait till we get bald-headed.' There is no convincing them; and any change for the better must come from without. A good deal of the evil is due to want of occupation of mind. They have none of the sports of young men in these densely populated regions of London. The consequence is—for human nature will have something to relieve the tedium of existence—the thoughts turn to love, instead of cricket and football. Recreation grounds—that is, playgrounds, not disused burial-grounds—will tend to prevent their flowing prematurely in this channel. And there is another movement tending in the same direction, of which I am about to speak; but for the present necessity I am persuaded a legal limitation is indispensable. We have lately been paternal: let us be paternal a step further, to save the youth of England. These marriages are as bad as anything which has recently been brought under our notice—in fact they are a part of the same unpleasant subject. I would make a limit of age, below which it would be illegal to marry. That this might not be evaded, I would subject any of the clergy who should marry those outside their proper jurisdiction to heavy penalties; for false statements as to age, and marriages without the knowledge of parents, can be stopped only in this way. I would make it incumbent on the clergy marrying people within their own district to assure themselves that they really reside at the address given, and that it is a *bonâ-fide* residence. It would be a good plan to require a term of twelve months, as this is the period that gives a settlement under the Poor Law, and such a provision is not to be overlooked by those about to marry. I would also make it a clerical duty to ascertain by birth certificates that both parties are of full age; and all this ought to be equally incumbent upon Registrars, and Nonconformist ministers, as upon clergy of the Establishment. It should not be lawful in great town parishes, with a number of subdivisions, for marriages to be celebrated in any district church of the parish: they should be performed only in the church of the district where one or both of the couple reside, and, in case of one, this should always be the would-be husband's parish, for it is his immaturity that is most to be guarded against. In the case of unconsecrated buildings of the Church of England I would remove the absurd restriction by which marriages are forbidden, while allowed in every registered Nonconformist chapel or Registrar's office; for it is this unjust inequality of the law that takes out of the knowledge of the clergy the most important matter with which, by advice and influence, they could possibly concern themselves. It is this iniquitous and vexatious rule that makes many of the clergy helpless to restrain abominations of which the law causes them to be kept in ignorance. Those unhappy boys who are married behind their Vicar's back would not dare to present themselves to his face, for they know very well he would point-blank refuse to marry them. If the duty of investigation should be too onerous for the clergy, it might well be devolved upon the police: the fee, however, for performing marriages is quite high enough to compensate for the additional trouble. False declarations of age I would make penal, and the marriages of the persons guilty of them null and void. If it could, by means thus roughly indicated, be made impossible for the marriages of infants to take place, the legislature would put a powerful check upon early seductions, since young people could no longer resort to the cloak of matrimony."

Of fifteen marriages taking place at —— Church in an East London Parish on a Monday in August, 1886, the following instances are worthy of remark.

	AGE.		
NO.	MAN.	WOMAN.	REMARKS.
1	19	18	
2	22	21	Private in foot regiment.
3	19	18	Girl looked 16 only.
4	24	22	Heavily pregnant.
5	22	18	Man out of work.
6	22	21	Pregnant.
7	19	17	
8	26	24	Heavily pregnant.

The rest were between 27 and 35.

The following is the report of the scene

that took place at the celebration of the rites of holy matrimony :—

"Inside the church there was a noisy mob; obscene jests were freely shouted out, and every minute they became coarser and more objectionable as the brides and bridegrooms became more intoxicated. One old lady, reeling about, was singing a Salvation Army tune set to a filthy jargon about the joys of married life, whilst some of the bridegrooms were shouting one to another to come and have another —— swig of beer; in fact, two couples had to be married half an hour after the rest because the happy bridegrooms had 'gone for a booze' and could not be found.

"It is a striking fact that out of all the fifteen couples only one had any holiday clothes to wear for such an important occasion. All the rest were in old working clothes, and some in rags. None had any witnesses with them, each couple signing one another's marriage certificate.

"After waiting till a quarter to twelve, the ceremony began. The Curate read all the names of the men first, and gabbled with them through their part, afterwards doing the same with the women, interlarded with a few remarks like this: 'Now then, ——, you are not saying it after me; you will have to say it by yourself if you ain't careful.' Or to another it would be: 'Say *I will*, and not *yes*, you idiot!' While this was proceeding the few who had strolled in to see the weddings were indulging in filthy jokes and suggestive actions quite openly, with no more respect for the house of God than if it was a stable.

"The church itself is in a shocking dirty and dilapidated state. One window near the altar, containing twenty-eight panes of glass, has thirteen broken; the dirty plaster is peeling from the walls, and nearly half the ceiling has fallen, leaving the bare rafters exposed to view.

"After the ceremony all adjourned to the nearest public-house except one young couple, who stood outside the church gazing stupidly about. I spoke to them, and asked if they lived close handy, but the young man said: 'I ain't got er place to go to yet; my old man don't know as I'm married, no more does 'er old woman—do she, Nell? We've got married on the sly.' After chatting for some few minutes, his girl wife said to him: 'The parson does chuck it of his chest, don't he, Bill?' And Bill answered with an oath: 'Well, and wot ther —— —— do you want for sevenpence halfpenny?'"

To Bank Holidays may be attributed a portion of the origin of this evil. "So far," writes the clergyman already quoted, "so far from canonizing Sir John Lubbock, if there be any opposite process I would ruthlessly apply it to him, for most of the premature marriages are his doing."

The other cause of the evil of reckless and premature marriage is the unloveliness and restrictions of the working man's home. Weary lads, without mental or physical resources, swarm from the alley hive before a stock of honey has been laid in for winter use. As a natural result there is a married pauper class, growing in numbers, who drag along during the summer with hopping, "hob-jobbing," and casual labour, depending for subsistence in winter time on the rates and on the charity that maintains and propagates the evils it blindly hopes to extinguish.

Zulus, Basutos, Amatongas, and other varieties of "poor heathen" pursue a different practice. It is attended with success. Every girl is the equivalent of so many cattle, and unless the swain can produce them, in exchange for his bride, he may live and die a bachelor. Kimberley diamonds are delved for by ebony Corydons labouring for the Phillises waiting for them throughout the length and breadth of the uplands south of the Zambesi. The bottomless rottenness of English cant prefers the fiction of a marriage tie with the facts of filth and infidelity, to enforced abstention from undertaking impossible responsibilities, at all events with the sanction of the State. It is not too late to place legislative obstacles in the way of unions repugnant to a true sense of purity, hostile to national interests, and fraught with evil to the living and to generations unborn, by demanding from male minors evidence of means, before undertaking the burden of family life.

Criminal and pauperised classes with low cerebral development renew their race more rapidly than those of higher nervous natures.

Statesmen idly stand by, watching in such moments as they can spare from the strife of party the victory of battalions destined to misery and crime over the struggling army of the prudent and the self-controlled. Birth into certain quarters of London is birth into an environment from which there is no escape. At three years old baby lips lisp oaths so bestial as to be coarse in the betel-stained mouths of the crew of a Coromandel *dhoney*. At six, little girls are initiated by their mothers into practices so loathsome the gorge rises at the thought. At ten, girls and boys alike are unclean spirits limited in their power for evil only by their abilities. Dynasties of criminals and paupers hand down from generation to generation hereditary unfitness for the arts of progress and all that brings greatness to a nation, and engage themselves in warring against all forms of physical and moral order. Where a man is criminal himself, the cause of crime in others, and the begetter of criminal posterity, it seems to be an act of mere self-protection on the part of this generation to segregate him. No less is it an act of justice to the next generation to take such measures as will, in conformity with enlightened public opinion, prevent him from tainting posterity with the pledges of his affection. In Eastern countries this matter could be discussed with greater ease. English convention forbids the discussion of detail which would otherwise be desirable. A Parliamentary vote to meet the cost of shutting up for life confirmed criminals cannot, however, bring a blush to any cheek. A woman of New York belonging to the criminal class died at a great age. She had spent forty years of her own life in prison. Investigation was made into what is termed her "life history," and it was found that over a hundred of her descendants had at one time or another abused the protection of the American Eagle. This may be an extreme example, but it is obvious that economy would have resulted to the American Republic from a luxurious but compulsory hospitality being accorded to the lady in question for the term of her natural life, from the time when her proclivity for crime became so marked as justly to deserve the epithet Habitual. Were criminals segregated for life after repeated conviction, posterity would, at all events, manufacture most of their own crime, instead of receiving from us so handsome a legacy as that which is now being prepared. Such a course would be costly, and would not lend itself to statistics. We could not count the gain, with precision. Diminution of crime and pauperism would result, but in unknown quantities. What is hit is History, what is missed is Mystery.

The following advertisement from the *Times* is the result of a type of outrage to be perpetrated by any healthy and impecunious curate with a light heart, with the sanction of the Church, and with the blessing of conventional society :—

"An urgent and earnest appeal is made on behalf of a widow and six young children, who, by the sudden death of the husband—a clergyman—are left penniless. Will some kind hearts come forward either to adopt or contribute towards the education and maintenance of the children, or aid the poor widow in her bitter hour of need? The highest references and full particulars can be given, and contributions," &c.

Teachers of men who incur direct money liabilities they are unable to discharge are unfrocked. Indirect responsibilities to unborn children, to be redeemed in case of death by an unknown public, are accepted with complacency, since the conventions of cant do not reprobate the offender with the illwill of respectable society. Daughters may go to the streets and sons to Dartmoor as the consequence of selfish marriage, but the smug maxims governing what the clergyman termed " the so-called nineteenth century " not only condone, but encourage the offence of bringing into the world creatures for whom there is no reasonable prospect of either healthy or happy existence. With such examples to the common people, what hope is there of driving home the need of thrift and common prudence? On the clergy rests, to a large degree, responsibility for the reckless fecundity which is part of our national offending. Healthy public opinion may well be brought to bear on the cruelty of precept and example alike inflicted on the poor by so many of our pastors.

The practice of the Roman Catholic Church

in regard to this matter is stated by his Eminence Cardinal Manning as follows:—

"As to early marriages, the Church has no special laws. It does not discourage them, under conditions of common prudence, knowing the danger of opposing them.

"It is a balance of dangers. On the one side the danger of want and destitution: on the other, the danger of demoralization. We fear the latter more than the former, and I believe Ireland shows that we are right and Bavaria confirms it. But then we have more hold over the married than over the unmarried, and they come to us more readily in their troubles. A home, however poor, is a fixture. The unmarried are untraceable, and cannot be so easily known and watched over. They go to and fro. This will not apply to the general population in the same degree.

"My belief is, that the destruction of home-life among the people comes from the extreme right of property and the excesses of political economy, and, I must add, the devouring drink trade."

The practice of the Jewish community is

stated by the Rev. S. Singer to be as follows:—

"Nowhere, perhaps, are the evils consequent upon that system (of premature marriages) more acutely felt than among my own co-religionists.

"Some allowance must, of course, be made for the Eastern origin of the Jewish people. Something must also be set down to the fact that early marriages are looked upon with a considerable degree of favour by many of our most trusted teachers, ancient and modern, who regard the practice as a preventive against greater evils. The comparatively high standard of family morals among Jews no doubt justifies this anticipation to a certain extent. Still the question is, whether there is anything incompatible between prudence and public morality, and the more far-sighted among us would fall in with the judicious conclusion of the Talmud, which in an exposition of the sequence of verses in Deuteronomy xx., 5, 6, 7, observes: 'Here the law teaches us a lesson for the guidance of human society, and indicates that a man should first build his house and plant his vineyard and *then* take a wife, as if to say no marriage should be undertaken unless the means of support are at hand and a foundation has been laid for the fulfilment of the responsibilities of marriage.'

"You ask me what is the practice of the Jewish community in regard to the marriages of male minors in the event of their being unable to support the responsibilities of a family?

"There is, in fact, no fixed procedure, nor any regulation on the subject. Our Board of Guardians and Lying-in Charities assist women in their confinements. At circumcision further help is frequently forthcoming from the benefactions of our richer brethren, contributed for that purpose at the circumcision of *their* sons.

"A public institution of ours, the Jews' Hospital and Orphan Asylum, receives, educates, etc., the children of indigent parents after election by the subscribers. Our Free Schools have long given education of a very high order to the children of the poor, and through the generosity of a few philanthropic members of our body, notably the Rothschild family, the poorest among our pupils are supplied with food and clothing.

"The Jewish Board of Guardians apprentices boys and girls to various trades. The synagogues at stated periods distribute gifts in money and in kind. Many families are assisted to emigrate. There is, indeed, a general objection to giving pecuniary or other relief to young people capable of work, but the objection usually breaks down in the presence of evident and pinching want.

"With deep regret I confess that the innate benevolence of the Jewish race is at times itself the cause of the improvidence we all deplore.

"In my visits to the poor in the East of London I am often staggered at the blind rashness with which young people have rushed into marriage. The people to whom I refer have mostly come from foreign parts (although instances of early and imprudent marriages are not rare even in England). It is not an uncommon thing to find parents of 19 or 20 arriving here from Russia and Poland with two or three children, and without any means of supporting themselves and their offspring. Herein lies, I hold, the chief cause of that grinding poverty with which the Jews as a race are afflicted.

"The popular notion concerning the wealth of Jews is a fallacy which ought by this time to be exploded. The idea owes its origin in part to the presence of a few opulent families among us, but still more, perhaps, to the circumstance that we do not parade our distress before the world, and, while helping to support the public burdens, relieve our own poor independently of parish, and as a rule, also, of Gentile assistance.

"A little practical experience of the wretchedness our brethren live in would dispel the popular fancy regarding the wealth of the Jews, and would carry home the conviction that for by far the greater part of that wretchedness nothing is answerable but the number of early, premature, and imprudent marriages that take place among us.

"Even the beneficent effects of sobriety, industry, and the strongest family affections, are to a great extent neutralized from this cause alone.

"For whatever you can do to throw the

light of reason upon a practice productive of immense present, and incalculable future, misery, you ought to earn the gratitude of all who desire the permanent amelioration of the condition of the poor."

The Nonconformist bodies appear to be free from the charge of encouraging reckless and improvident marriages.

Limitation of families is a subject that has been spoiled by Mr. Bradlaugh and his colleagues. In the public mind there is an indissoluble alliance between deliberate restriction and aggressive atheism. There is not, it is true, on the surface any necessary affiance between the two. Possibly Mr. Bradlaugh and Mrs. Besant are people who have lived a generation too soon. The arguments against them were employed against Sir J. Y. Simpson, when chloroform was first administered in cases of childbirth. An all-wise Creator, it was said, ordained that women in their travail should travail in pain, and it would be impious to impair by anæsthetics the full force of so wise a provision. A similar line of reasoning might have been adopted against cropping the hair. Interference with nature is the condition of civilization. It is not natural to exist between a paving-stone and a canopy of smoke. But this is the condition of millions of poor souls who, under brighter circumstances, could enjoy the gentians of the Alps or the waters of the Riviera as keenly as their critics. As things are marching now, non-interference with nature is hurrying the nation to disorder by the wholesale production of people who rarely wash or change their clothes; who are subject to prolonged and irregular intervals between meals; who breathe tainted air in insanitary hovels, and who are in a more decrepid condition of mind and body than the heathen in foreign parts before we extended to them the advantages of brandy, Bible, and the diseases of advanced civilization.

In 1885 a Committee sat at the Mansion House to inquire into the causes of permanent distress in London, and the best means of remedying the same.

The Committee was representative, and contained some distinguished names. The following forms part of the Report:—

" There appear to be grounds for believing that the increase of the population (with or without marriage) is greatest in those classes which have the least means of supporting large families. And this increase is due quite as much to the early age at which many become parents as to the number of children brought into the world without any provision for their maintenance. In the result it would appear that the undue increase of the population is closely connected with extreme destitution. The question of early marriages is a very important one as regards both morality and pauperism, and the matter might be profitably investigated."

After so specific an opinion, it might be presumed that the Committee came to deal with the question of remedies for permanent distress in London. Not a bit of it. The subject was ignored. The logical corollary of such an expression of opinion would have been a recommendation that an inquiry (by Royal Commission or otherwise is desirable) into the effect of early and reckless marriages as well as into the connection between the undue increase of population and destitution.

It is desirable, therefore, in order to sterilize the unfit—

1. That the legal age of marriage should be raised.

2. That reckless marriages should be prevented —

(a) By requiring from male minors previous to the celebration of marriage evidence of ability to maintain a family.

(b) By an Act of Parliament enabling clergy and registrars to refuse to act for reasons stated.

3. Permanent segregation by the State of criminals after repeated conviction.

4. Change of example and precept by the clergy, and the creation of a healthy public opinion in regard to the responsibility of adults for children begotten by them.

5. An inquiry by Royal Commission into the effect of early and reckless marriages, and their connection with destitution.

Notes to Chapter III.

A.

Numbers and proportions per cent. of persons married who were not of full age in West and East London in the year 1884; and of those married in the Church of St. James the Great in Bethnal Green in 1884 and 1885:—

Districts.	Marriages.	Not of Full Age.		Percentage of Married not of full age.	
		Males.	Females.	Males.	Females.
St. George, Hanover Square ...	1421	22	147	1·55	10·34
Bethnal Green ...	2587	380	926	14·69	35·79
Group of West Districts ...	6490	249	891	3·84	13·73
Group of East Districts ...	6945	660	1942	59·0	27·96
Church of St. James the Great in Bethnal Green — 1884	647	70	169	10·8	26·1
— 1885	626	75	185	12·0	29·4

B.

Annual Birth and Death rates in St. George, Hanover Square, and Bethnal Green, in ten years 1871-80, and in 1885 :—

Districts.	Annual Birth Rate.		Annual Death Rate.	
	Ten Years 1871-80.	1885.	Ten Years 1871-80.	1885.
St. George, Hanover Square ...	24·24	20·02	20·28	20·09
Bethnal Green ...	41·75	39·93	23·87	21·65

Note.—The death-rates in these Districts are not corrected for deaths in Public Institutions.

Marriages of Male Minors in

	Italy.	France.	England & Wales.	Prussia	Austria.
1882.					
Total number of marriages...	224,041	281,060	174,169	217,239	183,378
Marriages of Males under 20 years	2,595	6,901	5,093	226	—
,, ,, 24 ,, ,,	—	—	—	—	41,490
1883.					
Total number of marriages	—	—	—	220,748	176,016
Marriages of males under 20 years	—	—	—	156	—
,, ,, 24 ,, ,,	—	—	—	—	34,997

ILLEGITIMATE BIRTHS IN

Years.	Italy.		France.		Germany.		England & Wales.		Austria.		Hungary.	
	Total Births.	Illeg. Births.	Total Births.	Illeg. Births.	Total Births	Illeg. Births.	Total Births.	Illeg. Births.	Total Births.	Illeg. Births.	Total Births.	Illeg. Births.
1880	957,900	71,079	920,177	68,227	1,696,175	151,042	881,643	42,542	911,899	125,988	588,424	46,702
1881	1,081,125	79,508	937,057	70,079	1,682,149	150,883	883,642	43,120	915,145	124,281	594,414	47,139
1882	1,061,094	79,643	935,566	71,305	1,702,348	156,526	889,014	43,155	957,180	130,620	612,062	49,631
1883	—	—	—	—	—	—	—	—	*858,832	124,141	—	—

* Excluding Croatia and Slavonia.

C.

In 1884 14,818 men married under age in England, and 74,004 at the age of 21.

The practice of marriage by men under age has increased since 1841 from 4·38 per 100 to 7·25 in 1884.

In 1884, out of 2,587 marriages celebrated in the parish of Bethnal Green (area 755 acres, population 126,961), 380 were men not of full age.

During the same period in the parish of St. George's, Hanover Square (1,943 acres, 149,748 population), 1,421 marriages were celebrated, out of which 22 men were not of full age, that is to say the marriages of men under age in Bethnal Green are about ten times as numerous as in St. George's, Hanover Square.

CHAPTER IV.

EMIGRATION.

THERE is no subject relating to the well-being of the community in regard to which it is easier to generalise than the question of emigration. At first sight it seems as though emigration, and enough of it, were a panacea for the greater portion of the national evil caused by the pressure of our population. When, however, the subject is analysed in detail, it is found to be wedged round with a variety of political and economical difficulties, to be grappled with only by the community as a whole.

It is an axiom among those who are accustomed to apply themselves to matters relating to the well-being of their fellow countrymen, that the truest philanthropy is that in which the capital expended is returned. The enterprises of the late Mr. George Peabody and of Sir Sydney Waterlow are but examples of the truth of this general observation; and, unless it could be shown that money expended, either by individuals or by the nation, in facilitating discriminate emigration is either directly or indirectly reproductive, I should not include the subject of emigration as one of the means of liquidating our national debt.

The attitude adopted towards the subject of emigration varies according to the situation and interests of the observers. In England the question has been regarded almost exclusively from the philanthropic point of view. The spectacle of congested cities, of the thousands of unemployed, and the always shameful, because unnecessary, scenes of hundreds of able-bodied men clamouring at the dock gates for work which does not exist, has directed public attention to the feasibility of removing these unfortunates to another land, as an effective method of extirpating evils which are continually under process of generation.

One result of these philanthropic intentions has been to create in late years, in the Anglo-Saxon colonies, and in the United States— which is the saucer into which the European cup has overflowed since 1820—a feeling of repugnance and dread of large schemes of immigration, measurable only in intensity with the sentiment excited in Australia, or in South Africa in past times, when the mother country reversed the policy of the pelican, by feeding her colonies, not with the best of her blood, but with the rejected elements of her people. That this sense of wrong at the idea of Britain shedding her paupers on other lands is in existence, and is growing, there can be no question. We are met, therefore, with the initial fact that, whatever may be the destination of the pauper population of our great cities, our colonies not only will not encourage its transfer to their own shores, but will resist by every means in their power any misguided attempts in that direction.

The recent action of the American Government in regard to the introduction of pauper immigrants is well-known. At Castle Garden, the landing place of the immigrants to New York, an investigation is made by officers of the Customs Department as to the ability of the immigrants to pay their passages to the interior of the country, and to support themselves for a reasonable period of time. The result of this examination has been still further to diminish British emigration for the year 1885, the falling off in that year being 38,915, as compared with 1884. It is impossible not to sympathise with those beyond sea who decline to allow the Anglo-Saxon colonies to be treated as receptacles for the failures and for the unfit of British industrial life. That this feeling is deeply rooted needs no demonstration. Of its justice no facts can be more telling than the analysis of a given number, say, of the London unemployed who are candidates for emigration. During the winter of 1884-5, I happened to be brought closely in contact with about 6,000 unemployed men in the East End, and I have no hesitation in expressing my conviction that not more than $4\frac{1}{2}$ per cent. of their number were eligible for a new life in the colonies. A large proportion of these 6,000 were men who had, during a comparatively recent period of time, come to London in search of work; and it is remarkable that the small proportion of those who were adjudged by competent authorities as fit for emigration had, for the most part, but lately left the country districts.

These two facts, therefore, of colonial repugnance to receive the surplus population of British cities, and the unfitness of the majority of those whose presence forms a burden and danger to our social life, indicate that if the question of emigration is to be regarded as a remedial agent, and from a national point of view, the remedy must be applied before the individuals to be emigrated have sunk into the semi-nomadic conditions of casual labour in the great cities; before habits of continuous application have been lost, and before *physique* and *morale* alike are injured beyond hope' of repair.

If these conclusions are accepted as tenable it is clear that the appeals for support made by some of the Emigration Societies are based on ignorance of the facts. The following extract from the prospectus of the

National Association for Promoting State-Directed Colonization is an excellent example of the injury that may be done by unhealthy generalities expressed in philanthropic English. The Association enjoys the advantage of seventeen eminent Patrons, fifty-two Vice-Presidents, as well as a National Council of portentous proportions.

In East and South London, in many of our large cities and towns, and in some of the rural districts, there are accumulating rapidly-increasing masses of poverty-stricken, unemployed people. Perpetual anxiety, due to the terrible struggle for daily bread, enforced privation, overcrowding, miseries too many for enumeration, aggravated by corrupting influences surrounding the poor in all cities and manufacturing towns, are steadily visibly sapping and ruining the physical constitutions and energies of deserving, struggling, and helpless people, while discontent is leavening masses to whose doors education is now carried by the State. These people, now becoming educated, see luxury all around them. It is well that philanthropists, philosophers, and statesmen should ignore the palpable danger of such a condition of things? The evil is being intensified yearly by the increase in population, and by the rapid, though unavoidable introduction of labour-saving machinery in all departments of trade and agriculture. There is only one permanent remedy—a steady and continuous *drafting of our surplus population to our own Colonies*, where these people would become contented and useful to the British Empire, instead of remaining here, a starving, discontented menace to the mother-country.

Yet that remedy is quite beyond the reach of those in whose behalf State intervention is demanded—demanded not alone on grounds of charity or duty towards them, but in the interests of the whole community.

This Association has initiated a National Movement, with a view of inducing the Home and Colonial Governments to join hands in a work of mercy for our starving poor. The Colonies will gain by securing the supply of population they so much require; the people themselves will be infinitely advantaged by the removal. At home we have thousands with no work, no wages, no food, a constant burden upon our philanthropy and our rates. In our Colonies there are millions of untilled acres, the settlement and cultivation of which will provide an abundance of work, good wages, and cheap food. Yet, year after year, these thousands of willing but miserable people remain penned up in the courts and alleys of our cities and towns. All that is wanting is *the means to transplant these helpless ones from here to there*. They will go, if we will only enable them to do so.

The paragraphs quoted, italics included, are better adapted to defeat the efforts of the Federation League, to create a cry for separation, to stimulate the appetite for official obstruction, and to encourage socialism, than to carry into effect such practical measures as can be undertaken with due regard to political perspective.

Emigration has failed to touch, in recent years, the evils caused by the prevailing lack of employment, created by dwindling value and fluctuating volume of trade—and more especially by the enormous increase in the population of Great Britain. Such emigration as has taken place has been partly indiscriminate. During the year 1884, when 242,000 people of British origin left these islands, there was an influx during the same year, from all sources, of not less than 91,356. Of this number a large proportion were returned emigrants who had failed to make good their grip on the place selected for their attempt to obtain a livelihood.

Absence of authentic information as to the capabilities of the districts selected for settlement in the Colonies and elsewhere is the principal cause of these unsuccessful ventures. The statements of agents and others, who are chiefly concerned in procuring the transport of a certain tonnage of emigrants over lines of railway with land to sell, have led to the destruction of many hopes, and the permanent ruin of many lives.

The mere possession of 160 acres of land in the Colonies, without the essential knowledge, strength, or capital, is no greater boon than the acquisition of the now historical three acres and a cow is in England itself, when the possessor has neither time, ability, nor capital to develop the potential advantages of the land.

The glut of artisans in England represents a state of things prevailing nearly all over the world; and the transfer of carpenters' and builders' labourers to places where the demand for those forms of industry is below the supply available on the spot, is simply a re-arrangement of suffering, and is attended with no corresponding advantage.

A second cause of the comparative failure of recent emigration to cope with the volume of English distress, is the absence of adequate capital. There are in London, at this moment, sixty emigration societies and agencies bravely struggling with the task of meeting the necessity of the case, some of which have done and are doing good and noble work, however limited in extent that work may be.

It is not surprising that capitalists hold aloof from the expenditure of large sums of money where the competition for their support is so keen, the results of the work accomplished so comparatively insignificant, and where special and expert knowledge of the subject by the administration is by no means a matter of course.

From investigations made in 1885, it appears that twenty-five of the societies referred to succceeded in sending away no more than 3,500 individuals at a cost of £13,000. When it is remembered that not less than £4,500,000 are annually expended in public charities in the metropolis alone—which sum would provide £20 each for every one of the 200,000 human beings forming the submerged stratum of London life—the diversion of a moderate proportion of this enormous sum from the temporary relief of the necessitous to the permanent assistance of the able and the deserving, by means of emigration, would be, in all senses, a more productive use of the money.

Considerable efforts were made, in 1885, under good auspices, to induce the representatives of the societies to form a Bund or Central Council, in which information might be focussed, and to which the gifts or loans for emigration purposes of the charitably disposed might be entrusted. These efforts were not successful. Permanent officials withheld their approval.

Hitherto information in regard to the absorbtive capacities of the different colonies has been acquired by the disunited energies of societies or individuals. As there are ten Agents-Generals in London more or less interested in discouraging unwise emigration, superfluous work is involved both to them and to their correspondents and visitors, by the absence of a centre where exact information can be concentrated and dealt out.

An inquiry, however, at the Agents-Generals' offices does not appear to exhaust the well of truth as to the capacity of the colonies to receive suitable members of the British community. Democracy now reigns supreme in the Anglo-Saxon colonies. It is not surprising, therefore, that the protective policy, which is all but universal, extends not only to the exclusion of Chinese labour, but to all measures likely to lead to the reduction of wages.

The ambassadors of the colonies in question are debarred, therefore, from taking part in any movement which shall prejudice the interests of the wage-earning classes, who now form the bulk of colonial constituencies. That this is so, is, however, no reason why a serious and continuous effort should not be made to ascertain from month to month the actual condition of agricultural and other industry in and near every large town in every colony over which floats the British flag. I may, perhaps, adduce a practical instance of the importance and interest of local inquiry. The Representative of the Cape Colony is no longer in a position to promote emigration to South Africa, as the Cape Parliament has rescinded the emigration vote. Detailed inquiry in the Cape Colony, however, reveals the fact that, although some of the finest wheat in the world is grown in South Africa, the colony is importing food-stuffs for internal consumption to the amount of £1,020,000 a year, and that, consequently, the introduction of agricultural labour, at least sufficient to produce food-stuffs to that extent, would be of benefit to the Cape Colony, whatever the result might be to the mother country or to the emigrants themselves.

Take, again, the instance of New South

Wales. The following is an extract of a letter which appeared in the *Pall Mall Gazette* of 21st June, 1884 :—

NEW SOUTH WALES EMIGRATION.—The demand for agricultural labour of all sorts is still largely in excess of supply. The amount of genuine distress in the country may be estimated by the fact that the ' starving unemployed' have refused to accept 5s. a day on temporary Government relief works. The country is simply crying out for men, and it is pitiable to see the short-sighted efforts of those who are honestly attempting to dissuade English workmen from throwing in their lot there.

This is how Mr. Froude, in his new book "Oceana," describes Auckland, New Zealand :—

Eight shillings a day are the usual wages, and no able-bodied man who wants employment is ever at a loss to find it at that rate of pay. Beef is thought dear at sixpence a pound, bread is not dearer than in England, while fruit and vegetables are as much cheaper as they are superior in quality. The ' four eights' is an accomplished fact—eight hours to work, eight to play, eight to sleep, and eight shillings a day.

It is not surprising to read a little further on that the workmen " discourage immigration " as tending to lower their wages. This seems to be the result of extensive public works, affording unlimited employment, paid for by enormous loans raised at cheap rates in

England; and the workmen, being in the majority, can have their own way about the immigration.

It may, then, be fairly assumed that a case is made out for independent inquiry on the spot as to the condition of the local labour markets in the colonies. There is no doubt a continuous stream of valuable information pouring into the letter-boxes of the various emigration societies, and of individuals interested in the work of emigration. But the first step in a national scheme of emigration would be to combine these rivulets of knowledge, and to filter and compare them in order that they may be made of the greatest use to the community; and, furthermore, they require to be supplemented by the patriotic support of residents on the spot. If approached with tact and address, an individual or committee in every town of our colonial possessions will probably be found willing to support, by trustworthy and impartial monthly reports, the emigration bureau of centralised information, which it is to be hoped will be formed by the Government without loss of time.

Before such a bureau is in a position to

satisfy the demand for accurate knowledge, it would be necessary for one or two competent individuals to visit Australia and the Cape, properly accredited by the Government, for the purpose of enlisting the aid of volunteer helpers in the colonies, not only for the supply of trustworthy information, but for the honourable and patriotic purpose of advising and assisting those who leave England for the first time.

The present sources of knowledge do not exhaust the supply of facts; they are available to few; are often fragmentary, sometimes obsolete, and, not seldom, lead to indiscriminate emigration, and consequently to suffering, and disappointment.

At the present time information as to the industrial conditions ruling in British Colonies must be obtained from —

(a) The Agents-General of the Colonies.
(b) The Colonial Office publications, and the Annual Reports of the Governors of Colonies, presented to Parliament.
(c) Existing Emigration Societies.
(d) Individuals interested in the promotion of emigration from the United Kingdom.

The proposed Bureau * under the direction of the Colonial Office should be diligent in obtaining, sifting, and collating, from all available sources within the United Kingdom, intelligence of every description relating to the work; and should make it its business to supplement this intelligence by systematic efforts to obtain from trustworthy and non-political sources, in every town in every Colony, a monthly report as to the industrial and agricultural demand for labour in the town and district reported on.

As the political and industrial condition existing in the Anglo-Saxon Colonies differs in almost every case, the methods of obtaining the information desired must vary with the several peculiarities of the Colonies themselves.

The Government of Canada, having a vast extent of territory awaiting development, is not only ready, but eager, to further any steps which may lead to the introduction of suitable labour and additional capital. Sir John Macdonald has recently stated that his Government would be glad to co-operate

* An Emigrants' Information Office is now being organized by the Government.

with the proposed Bureau by causing the transmission to it, through the Minister of Agriculture, of regular, authentic, and responsible reports as to the needs of the different towns and provinces of the Dominion. This information would include confidential and semi-confidential intelligence, the publication of which might be, under some circumstances, undesirable, but the possession of which by the Bureau would be of value and importance.

The Cape Colony at the present moment presents not only an opening for a considerable number of judiciously selected agricultural immigrants, but the political effect of their addition to the Cape community would, in the opinion of men of all parties, be attended with happy results. In consequence, however, of the state of party politics at the Cape, it is impossible to ask, or to expect, that the Government of Mr. Sprigg will act in regard to the supply of information to the Bureau in the same manner as the Government of Sir John Macdonald. It is necessary, therefore, that other influences should be brought to bear. A recent visit to the Colony, in connection with a private scheme of colonization, enables me to say with confidence that there will be no difficulty in obtaining the assistance of responsible individuals who will supply in detail the information which cannot under present circumstances be supplied direct from Government sources.

With regard to the Australian Colonies something may be done by means of a circular dispatch, addressed to the Governors of the respective Colonies, inviting their support; but it will be necessary for a responsible agent, unconnected with politics, to visit Australia for the purpose of making permanent arrangements for the transmission of full, impartial, and regular reports. Dread of competition, displayed in an acute form in the Chinese Exclusion Acts, is equally hostile to any undertaking whatever which will have as an inevitable result the lowering of wages. On this ground the Governors of the Australian Colonies cannot be expected in their dignified and constitutional positions to identify themselves with measures openly repugnant to their Ministries, who represent constituencies the bulk of which are wage-earners, for these latter will undoubtedly be affected by the immigration of competitors from England and Scotland.

The information thus collected by the Bureau will require to be condensed, tabulated, and distributed. For the latter work the co-operation of the Post-Office Department should be ensured. It will also be well to publish information by means of semi-official printed notices to be displayed in selected rural and urban post-offices. The use of the telegraph for the dissemination of information should be allowed, at all events in cases of urgency and importance.

The advantage of this system over the present competitive muddle will be that the information supplied will be official, impartial, and true, instead of irresponsible, imaginative, or obsolete, as is now too often the case.

As the Bureau will occasionally obtain information of a deterrent character, warnings against the emigration of artizans or labourers to overstocked localities should form a special feature among the duties devolving on this Department.

Much has been said and written of late

about the federation of Britain with her Colonies. There is no way in which the true federation of the Empire can be more practically aided than by a union with our kin beyond sea for the purpose of developing their land and assisting ours. Work such as this lies beyond the province of a Government department. That the task is one capable of achievement, the example of the Cape Colony and of Canada—to which I shall allude further on—affords grounds for hope.

The next point indispensable to the success of a national scheme is the possession of funds. Bewildered by the multiplicity of demands for support, the English public has held aloof from the emigration movement. The subscription of £13,000 in one year from the whole of the metropolis does not suggest the idea of conviction being rooted in the public mind that the advantages, commercial or otherwise, of promoting wise emigration on a large scale, are such as to warrant serious efforts for the purpose. In the year 1884-5, £457,716 were expended in London on 92 Institutions for General Relief, Food Institutions, Loan Charities, and Homes. Investigation into the outcome of this expenditure, either to the individuals relieved, or to the nation at large, is disappointing to those who look for solid and permanent results.

Having regard, then, to the enormous sums laid out for transient advantages to suffering individuals, it does not seem Quixotic to expect that an appeal to the nation for means to convert those who now are, or will be, a burden to their fellow-countrymen, into self-supporting communities across the sea—consumers of large quantities of the products manufactured by those left behind—would fall on deaf ears.

The facility with which the cry for Imperial funds is raised is fascinating to those who do not reflect that any such addition to the burdens of the State paves the way to the assumption of tasks, not only more amenable to private enterprise, but which are in fact and essence foreign to the theory of constitutional government itself.

If, however, no case as yet has been made out for subventions from the State for colonisation, undertaken with the philanthropic object of relieving pressure at home, it is conceivable that cases have arisen, and even exist, where State colonisation may be a cheap and effective alternative to a military solution of burning questions. The old system of military settlers is now discontinued, but who can doubt that but for the settlements in South Africa of 1820-1857, ill-managed as they were—so far as the management attempted in the United Kingdom is concerned—the incessant and costly burdens laid on the mother country during the last twenty years would have been even heavier still. The British taxpayer has spent about £18,000,000 on South African wars since the year 1870, an expenditure caused by the neglect of Bacon's apothegm:—

"It is the sinfullest thing in the world to forsake or destitute a plantation once in forwardness; for, besides the dishonour, it is the guiltiness of blood of many commiserable persons."

The settlement of the Eastern Province in 1820, at the charges of the British exchequer, has again and again saved the vulnerable side of the Cape Colony from being "eaten up" by "man-slaying machines" from the east and north. This being so, the conclusion is irresistible that the wise expenditure by England during the last thirty years of a million of money for colonising purposes, would not only have saved the outlay of the greater part of the vast sum wasted in wars, which have settled nothing, and pleased no one but the contractors, but would have created a large and permanent demand for British manufactures.

The recent expedition to Bechuanaland, involving an expenditure of over a million sterling, has left a country the size of Spain to fortuitous development, and to the chances of Boer energies and leisure. Beyond the resources of private enterprise, the colonisation of Bechuanaland by Great Britain, at a cost of £125,000, not for the purpose of relieving home distress, nor even with the object of creating a new market for British trade, but to stock with settlers of British and loyal Dutch blood a land coveted by those who regard not their neighbours' landmark, in the opinion of those on the spot most competent to judge, would secure for the British taxpayer an assurance of peace and rest from which, under present circumstances, he is only too likely again to be disturbed. And when this disturbance does arise, it should be remembered that the sword cannot be effectively drawn 1,000 miles in the interior of Africa for half a quarter of a million of money. England has now assumed a responsibility for Bechuanaland which belongs to her whether she recognises or evades her inalienable engagements to white men and black. The alternative accordingly is offered either of making a moderate expenditure for a special purpose, which shall be as final in its way as was the cost of the colony of 1820, or of incurring liabilities which accumulate at compound interest while England sleeps.

Such an expenditure in Bechuanaland gratuitously made to the settlers chosen, would, in the course of time, pay itself. There was a married couple named Cawood who went, in 1820, to the Cape Colony, in the ship *John,* in Hazelhurst's party. There are now 500 descendants of the original Cawoods in the Cape Colony, consuming to the amount of £1,500 to £1,600 a year of British products. The annual profit to the mother country on the consumption of the Cawoods exceeds the original cost of their settlement by the British Government. While it cannot be expected that every couple will be as profitable or as prolific as the Cawoods, their debt to the Government of the day has been more than discharged by the stability they have contributed to the colony, by the work they have created for artisans and spinners in the old country, and by the indirect advantages of every kind, arising from their having taken root in South Africa. An old writer has said " that the planting of countries is like planting of woods, for you must take account to lose almost twenty years' profit, and expect your profit in the end."

The financial aid of the State should accordingly be sought only in such exceptional cases as those now presented by the Bechuanaland or Zululand problems, and then only as affording the cheapest and most effective means of meeting inalienable responsibilities incurred toward the country requiring settlement, and not in any sense from philanthropic motives, which, however laudable in the individual, have no place in the machinery of Government.

Such problems present the dilemma of cannon or colonisation; and as the cannon solution is more costly, less permanent, and is productive of ill-feeling all round, the other horn of the dilemma appears on the whole preferable.

The destination of emigrants is of the highest importance to the best interests of British commerce. In 1884, 155,280 people of British origin left for the United States, and when there, consumed, *per capita*, an average of 10s. worth of British manufactures, making an annual consumption of £77,640 of British goods. The same year, 44,255 left for Australia and New Zealand, where, according to the average scale of consumption ruling in Australia, they became at once annual customers for British goods to the amount of £352,000 per annum. In other words, two Australian immigrants, as customers to Great Britain, are equal to thirty-three subjects of the United States. An emigrant to South Africa is, commercially, six times more valuable than an emigrant to the States. That trade follows the flag is often said, but the force and extent to which the British flag is pursued by British trade is not so clearly a matter of common knowledge.

If the facts stated are sufficient to induce patriotic citizens to provide adequate funds for a considerable increase to discriminate emigration, it is clear that there must be some national body or council unconnected, as a whole, with any special interest, faith, or society. A national emigration Council should by no means engage in the details of sending emigrants away. To do so would involve the creation of yet another competitor in the bewildering crowd of claimants for public money. The function of the Council should be to receive funds from the public and distribute them impartially to societies and individuals who have proved themselves competent and economical in the transaction of previous emigration business. Representatives of the principal societies would naturally form an important part of the council, and the first step towards federation for executive purposes would thus be taken. All the existing associations are hampered for want of funds, and any legitimate means which would increase revenue without involving interference could not but be regarded with favour by them. The national council being, through the Bureau of Information, in full possession of the views and various needs of the Colonies, would either stimulate or check the outflow of labour as circumstances may demand, and reduce to a minimum the scandal and suffering caused by ignorance on the part of the emigrant himself.

The other objects of the council would be as follows :—

1. To place itself in constant communication with the Colonial Office in London, with the Agents-General, and with agents appointed for the purpose in the Colonies.

2. To obtain assistance from persons or societies in the Colonies, who will undertake to receive and place emigrants and their families.

3. And generally to ascertain from time to time the limits within which emigration from the United Kingdom can be conducted.

4. Having thus ascertained the possible "openings" for emigrants, to place such

openings at the disposal of the various existing local agencies.

5. To receive funds, and to distribute them among local agencies.

6. The council should not attempt to make centralisation take the place of the personal care and minute attention to details which smaller local associations alone can give, but leave them to adopt their own system of work, subject to such conditions as the council may from time to time think desirable.

7. The council itself not to undertake any emigration, but if it appears that the demand for emigrants at any time seems likely to be in excess of the supply, to organise new local committees to do the work.

The existence of a national council would also be of use in the following ways:—

a. As the channel of communication with the Imperial Government.

b. As the channel of communication with the Colonial Governments, and in particular to apply to them for (1) free or assisted passages; (2) reduced rail fares; (3) immigration agency in the Colonies, including further efforts to obtain openings for emigrants, and facilities on their landing.

And generally, the existence of such a council would be likely to inspire confidence in the charitable public, and thus to increase the subscriptions available for emigration.

• Although England is the only country in Europe to which a national scheme of emigration is either feasible or profitable, there are some points in the practice of other emigrating nations which are not without interest in the study of this question.*

GERMANY.

The influence of certain land systems in affecting emigration is shown by the province of Mecklenburg-Strelitz. The area is 1,130 English square miles, and the whole ownership of the territory is divided between the Grand Duke, feudal proprietors, and the corporations of certain towns, in the following manner—527 square miles to the Grand Duke, 353 to the nobles, and 117 to the town corporations. The population, although only 100 to

* The following details are the result of personal investigations on the Continent.

the square mile, is less in Mecklenburg-Strelitz than any other State of the German Empire; the average density of the population in which is 213 to the square mile. Owing to the manner in which the land is held, the emigration from Mecklenburg is proportionately to the population three times as great as is the case in Saxony, which is the State most densely populated in the Empire.

Emigration from Germany is discouraged, and when, as is the case in some parts of Mecklenburg, districts are depopulated, the discouragement by the Government is displayed by the adoption of strong measures. The principal causes of emigration from Germany are, undoubtedly, the fear of war, the hatred of military service, the crowded condition of every department of industry, and the immense competition for employment caused by the 160,000 soldiers who are yearly thrown on the world; and for whose sake, it is said on good authority, Prince Bismarck acquired for the State the control of the railways.

The comparative success of German emigrants, as compared with those of our own country, may be attributed to the facts—

firstly, that the standard of comfort in Germany is lower than that ruling in England; and, secondly, that as a family seldom or never emigrates without some small provision in the way of capital, the sufferings arising from pauper emigration are practically obviated. The German Government, like the English, take especial pains to ensure the comfort and well-being of the emigrants on board ship.

But the policy of protection, which in Germany is as comprehensive and far-reaching as the military system itself, is developing year by year. One of these developments is a provision which will shortly come into force, by which the steamers conveying German emigrants must be fitted in such a way as will conflict with the regulations laid down by the English Board of Trade, and which will consequently prevent the conveyance of German and English emigrants by the same vessel.

Emigration agents at Hamburg and Bremen have to deposit 18,000 marks in the hands of the Government, which are liable to forfeiture if by false and misleading representations they consign settlers to unhealthy parts of the world where success is impossible.

While the German Government discourages emigration as a whole, they are doing all they can to promote the settlement of their own recently acquired colonies.

New regulations of a restrictive nature will shortly be issued by Germany, and this being known stimulates emigration, for many towns of Germany are under martial law. Unmarried men can be ejected at twelve hours' notice, and married men at twenty-four hours' notice; a dangerous precedent for Germany, when it is remembered that there are now 23,000 immigrant Germans in London alone. The nations of Europe cannot fail to remember the action of Germany with reference to the Jews and Poles, on their eastern border, should occasion arise. It is not too much to say that half the emigrants from German ports are of the Jewish faith. They have an hereditary dislike to military service, and are more prone to apply themselves to commercial pursuits than to bear arms, though recent events in Bulgaria supply instances of an opposite nature.

The greatest depression in Germany is followed, as elsewhere, by the greatest emigration, and it is interesting to observe that the tax on corn already presses heavily on the lower classes.

The average actual number of young men drawn from the ordinary conditions of service in the army is 160,000, besides 5,000 who enter as volunteers for one year, and 5,000 for the marine.

The total population of the Empire of Germany in 1882 was 45,213,000; and 3,000,000 Germans have emigrated to the United States since 1820.

There is hardly any emigration either to British North America or to Australia; in 1881, for example, while 206,000 Germans went to the United States, only 286 went to British North America and 745 to Australia.

The loss by emigration from Germany is estimated at not less than £30,000,000, as the emigrants, when settled in their new country, are purchasers of German manufactures and produce to a very trifling extent; it need hardly be pointed out that this is not the case when Englishmen go to English colonies.

The military system is the means by which the German Government retain a hold on individuals and prevent able-bodied men from quitting the fatherland.

The Chancellor justifies his action in regard to the forthcoming restrictions and changes in the arrangements for shipping interests, by the plea that, as there must be a certain amount of emigration, it is well to keep it in German hands—that is in German ships.

Much trouble is caused to the German Home Secretary, as well as to the Imperial Commissioner for emigration matters, stationed at Hamburg (which gentleman is directly under the control of the Home Minister). The opinion of leading circles appears to be that it will be best to avoid an encouragement of whatever character as regards emigration, and consequently it has diminished within the last few years. The number of young Germans attempting to escape military duty is comparatively limited; statistics show the correctness of this statement.

In 1884 the emigrants carried with them about 20,000 children (under 10 years), who, of course, went with their parents. This proves that the majority of the 45,600 male emigrants (above 10 years) must have been married men, who had served their time in the army. The emigration of young men between the ages from 17 to 25 is strictly forbidden by German law; all vessels leaving Hamburg are watched by the police on this account.

There exists no Imperial Act regulating emigration matters, but almost all States have their local statutes, by which the transactions of emigration agents are supervised most carefully.

The following is an extract from the *Börsen Halle* of December 2, 1885 :—

"The local magistrate for the district of Aurich has informed all emigration agents within his district that such agents who distribute circulars inviting persons to emigrate, without having previously been requested to do so by persons wishing to emigrate, shall be deemed guilty of an illegal action, and if acting contrary to above instructions, shall lose their licenses. At the same time the agents are strictly ordered to abstain from taking part in any foreign colonisation scheme, and not to enter into any transaction for the purpose of obtaining emigrants for foreign countries."

The Imperial German Government has appointed an Imperial Commissioner, who has to supervise emigration from Germany, and who is stationed at Hamburg. This official has to make an annual report about emigration matters, which is to be laid before Parliament.

The normal increase to the population being about one per cent., the proportion of emigration is about one-third of the normal increase of the population.

It is impossible to leave this subject without remarking the great moral and physical good that has resulted from compulsory military service throughout Germany. The emigrants present signal examples of temperance, thrift, and energy.

The following letter from a gentleman high in the diplomatic service gives some interesting particulars as to German emigration :—

"From 1876-80 the number of emigrants averaged 33,971 in each year, of which 8465 went indirect, *i.e.*, from Hamburg to their destination through an intermediate port. In 1882, there were 113,221, of which

31,128 were indirect; 1883—89,465, of which 13,265 were indirect, and in 1884—91,603, of which 16,339 were indirect. The places to which these emigrants went were the United States, British North America, Mexico, Central America and West Indies, Brazil and the River Plate Republics, and other South American States, Africa, Asia, and Australia. In 1879, the number was 24,864, and in 1884—91,603. The two heaviest years were 1881-2, the numbers being 123,000 and 113,200 respectively. The emigrants are from all classes, the labouring class furnishing the largest contribution, and those without occupation coming next. The provinces of Pomerania, Prussia (East and West), and Schleswig-Holstein would appear to be the largest contributors. In 1884, of the total number of 75,264 direct emigrants, 71,843 went to the United States; 1,738 to Brazil, &c., 769 to Australia, 604 to other South American States, and 107 to Asia. Of persons over 10 years, in 1884, there were 45,638 male and 24,790 female, and from 1 to 10 years there were some 20,000. Of these, 33,059 were single men, 8,901 single females, and 14,206 families. The *raison d'être* for emigrating is difficult to say. The German authorities strenuously deny that the military system has any influence in promoting the desire, and quote in proof of this that the greater number of those going out of the country are time-served men, but assert that the real *raison d'être* is to better themselves, and urge in proof of this, that large numbers of the labouring class, who, not being able to attain to the luxury of a cottage and plot of land here, say, 'We will emigrate.' Yet the figures quoted show a very large number of single men;

of course, there are no means of verifying how many of these are time-served men. I have not the smallest hesitation in believing that the idea of rising in the social scale, and the magnificent will-o'-the-wisp idea of becoming a peasant proprietor, are two powerful motives in inducing them to emigrate, but without facts and figures, I cannot assert that military pressure—whatever I may believe—exercises any influence. I have known individual cases."

NORWAY.

There is a large relative emigration from Norway, which is mainly directed to the United States, to a very small degree to Canada, while none at all reaches the other English colonies. The principal cause is the want of agricultural employment, and the emigrants are therefore almost exclusively peasants and servant girls. Many of them are peasant proprietors, and realize the value of their small properties before leaving Norway, and do not, as is the case with a similar class in England, drift into the large towns. The population increases with considerable rapidity, but in Norway alone, among European countries, is the whole social question solved by emigration. There being no large towns, there is none of that magnetic attraction of a great mass which presents so difficult a problem in our own country. On the other hand, the standard of comfort throughout the country is lower than that prevailing in England, and there is comparatively no social or political discontent among the working classes.

There appears to be a general and intelligent understanding that the law of natural increase must be met by swarming to other hives, and not by political agitation for a readjustment of property. There is no discontent with the land system as it is, nor with the obligation to military service. Such pressure as does exist is that of want, and the minds of the people are not obscured by Socialistic teachings which inflame the residuum in countries of greater wealth.

The healthy character of Norwegian emigration is shown by the success attending the efforts of those who leave their country; secondary emigration being caused by those who, having succeeded in America, transmit funds to Norway, to enable their friends to join them in their new home; there is little or no pauper emigration, most of the people taking a little money with them. Their standard of comfort at home being low, they are not disappointed with the inevitable hardships and privations attending pioneer effort in a settlement; it may be added that there are few or no unemployed artizans.

EMIGRATION FROM NORWAY DURING THE YEARS 1880-4.

	To America.	To other places.	Population of Norway.
1880	20,212	597	1,910,000
1881	25,976	20	1,915,000
1882	28,804	16	1,913,000
1883	22,167	31	1,914,000
1884	14,776	13	1,923,000

The increase of population for the years 1881-4 was about 96,000, and the actual emigration for the same period, 91,803.

All emigration is under police control; each emigration and steam-ship agent gives securities for 20,000 kröne, as a guarantee for good treatment on board ship; this deposit has occasionally been forfeited for misrepresentation, and from various causes, but it forms a substantial guarantee of the good faith of the emigration agent, and for decency and good treatment on board ship. Before leaving, every emigrant has to appear before the police, in order to prove that he has satisfied the obligation of military service; the police also take an account of how much money the emigrant takes out of the country, and it may be well here to add that the definition of emigrant in Norway is " a person who leaves his country to better himself, and who travels at a reduced rate, under regulations enacted and maintained by the police."

There are no private societies, nor any private enterprise, to promote emigration, the feeling of the people being so strongly in its favour. The attitude of the Government is somewhat hostile, and on a recent occasion the circulars of emigration agents have been stopped in the post.

The effort of Norwegian statesmen is directed towards the reduction of taxation, and thus to render emigration unnecessary. There is a graduated taxation on bachelors and married men; they are divided into four classes, and assessed for taxation in inverse proportion to the number of their families.

The Gothenburg system is now being tried in many small towns, and it is so great a success that it came into force in Christiana in January, 1866.

The sobriety thus introduced into the habits of the Norwegians, which it is not too much to say has been induced by wise legislation, has seriously and favourably affected the character and qualifications of the emigrants.

HUNGARY.

The Hungarian Government deters emigration, by inducing migration to, and colonisation of, State lands, on which free schools and churches are given gratis; the payment for land is spread over fifteen years, and immunity from taxation granted for a similar period.

There is little or no distress among Hungarian peasantry, but there is considerable ignorance; and the consequence is that they have been misled by the statements of the beauty of America, and the facilities offered there for luxurious existence without the need of work. The increase in population is very small. Hungary is an agricultural country, and her interest, therefore, is in free trade.

The greater number of emigrants consists

of indebted smaller country farmers, ruined by bad harvests and heavy State and communal taxes; the others are Jews, poor labourers, and a few town people, especially female servants. The causes of emigration in many cases are want of work, and in some parishes over-population. Provisions against emigration are laid down in law, Article 38 of the year 1881. The title of this law is "Of the Emigrational Agencies." There is no way of directly prohibiting the emigration of citizens, but in the case when the emigrant has not yet fulfilled his obligation for military service—the Government finding that the greater number of emigrants do not leave their native country spontaneously, but are induced there by agents who buy up cheaply the little property of such emigrants, and only try to induce the largest possible number to emigrate, getting their commission on the number; on account of these reasons the legislature has devised measures against the agencies providing :—

"That no one is allowed to enter into contract relating to emigration with people who want to emigrate but those who are furnished by the Minister of the Interior with a license for agency.

"Anybody acting as agent without license can for each act be punished with a fine not exceeding 300 florins, and with imprisonment for a period not exceeding two months."

Agents are not allowed to have any business intercourse with foreign agents or agencies without the license of the Minister of the Interior.

Agents are under the control of the authorities, and have to give notice of each case of emigration which has been negotiated by them.

The contracting party can at any time withdraw his obligation, he only being bound to refund to the agent the out-of-pocket expenses incurred in drawing up the contract, as well as any sums advanced, and the eventual travelling expenses laid out for the party.

The agent can only be furnished with a license if he be an Hungarian subject. The Minister of the Interior can refuse to grant the license, even if the person requesting the right of agency answers to all requirements of the law, and he is also authorised to retract the license at any time. The licenses expire in one year, and must be renewed after the expiration of that period.

If evidence is furnished against an agent having committed fraud or deceit, or that he has meditated the emigration of such persons as have not yet fulfilled their military service, or of persons under age without the agreement of their parents or guardians, the whole of the caution money of the agent becomes at once forfeited.

POPULATION CENSUS, DECEMBER 31ST, 1880.

Male	7,799,276
Female	7,939,192
Total	15,738,468

1881. Births ... 604,262 ... Deaths ... 492,727
1882.   „   ... 708,011 ...   „   ... 571,854

It is needless to give the results of the investigations I have made in other European countries, as Germany, Norway, and Hungary; each throw some light on the emigration question, and afford in certain particulars examples to imitate. While France is a warning to deter in everything that relates to colonization, the standard work of M. Leroy Beaulieu, "De la colonisation chez les peuples modernes," is an exhaustive and philosophic treatise on the causes of success and failure in the art of colonization.

The practice of England herself is not without interest. While the State concerns itself with parental regard in seeing that the statutory size of the emigrant's bed, as provided in the Passengers Act, is carefully adhered to, it ignores the depredations of unprincipled people who, by dexterous evasion of the law, ruin the lives and destroy the hopes of thousands yearly. While the State is careful to ensure comfort, and even luxury, to the poor emigrant during his passage, she has hitherto neglected the more important question of advising as to his destination, and of care as to the character of the influences that have led him to quit this country.

If England cares little as to why the poor emigrant leaves the country, and is at no pains to equip him with the latest and best information, or to direct his courage and his energies into the best available channels, she is punctilious in assuring him provision of three tons of cubic space during his passage, and in seeing that the dietary scale provided by law is carried out.

The Passengers Act of 1855 is now obsolete and needs revision. Under the shelter of its provisions astute and unprincipled men practise on the credulity of the poor, and actually convert provisions designed to protect the duly licensed passenger broker and his clients into the means of evading the law, and misleading, in the light of day, hundreds and thousands of ignorant and innocent victims. A few simple alterations would secure a marked improvement. Cases have occurred at the Mansion House Police Court within a recent period, where complainants have sought advice from the magistrates as to means of obtaining redress for misstatements with reference to passages. As this law at present stands, the Board of Trade and the emigration officers acting under them are powerless to assist the emigrants.

This difficulty arises from the 4th, 66th, and 71st sections of the Passengers Act of 1855. From the 4th section it will be seen that the Act never contemplated embarkation elsewhere than in the United Kingdom; and from the 66th and 71st sections it will be seen that the words "from the United Kingdom" raises a difficulty which cannot be got over.

Any future amendment of the Passengers Act should follow the lines of the Netherland law on emigration, which, in Article 7, sets forth :—

> "Any person undertaking, either on his own account or as agent, to convey Dutch or foreign emigrants from the Netherlands, or a place out of Europe, shall, notwithstanding whether the embarkation takes place in a Netherland or a foreign port, previously provide real or personal bail, as a guarantee for the fulfilment of the conditions," &c.

Article 23 provides also that persons referred to in the first part of Article 7 should give security, &c.

Article 22 also prohibits persons who are qualified according to the Act from advertising in newspapers, posting up bills, hanging out boards, &c., or taking any means whatever for making it known that they are emigrant agents; and giving the police authority to deal with such cases is a wise precaution, and would put a stop to an immense amount of imposition being practised on emigrants.

Already our own colonial dependencies do

more than half as much business with us in a year as all the rest of the world put together. In fourteen years the imports of British goods by our four largest colonies have nearly doubled, and if the same rate of progress be maintained, in twenty-one years the internal trade of the Empire will be worth as much as the trade of the United Kingdom with the rest of the world. Looking at the falling-off in other directions, it would seem as though the Colonies are the only quarters to which we can look with assurance for continued increase, and there is nothing so certain to stimulate that trade as a new and vigorous effort to create our own custom. In fact, the question is no longer whether we shall do it, but how is it to be done? and the line of least resistance to the desired end will assuredly be found in a new and cordial determination to understand the needs and to gratify the legitimate desires of our fellow subjects across the sea. Federation may be formulated by the politicians, but the essence and reality of federation must exist in the hearts of the people, or the word is but a tinkling cymbal and sounding brass.

The permanent officials of the Treasury have a light-hearted manner of dealing with permanent distress. When it was brought to their notice that a certain measure of relief to the unemployed might be effected by the establishment of an Information Bureau, this was the reply : " If any additional Government-aid beyond that which can be afforded by the present machinery of the Colonial Office and Board of Trade is to be rendered for this purpose, my Lords think the least objectionable form it could take would be a revival of the small grant of from £50 to £100 per annum which used to be made by Parliament for the distribution of circulars relating to colonization amongst intending emigrants."*

In reply to this communication, the Colonial Office remark, with justice, " That their Lordships appear not to appreciate the importance of the arrangement proposed."

Not long afterwards Parliament voted £1,200 to protect the rights of the Crown in regard to the Lauderdale Peerage!

* The Information Bureau is now being organized, and will shortly be opened to the public.

It is needless precisely to estimate the money gain to Great Britain by the creation of a national scheme of emigration. Combined and fuller information collected in part, and distributed wholly by the State; the creation of a National Emigration Council and Intelligence Department; the provision of funds by the community; the adoption by the State of Colonizing schemes as alternatives to Military measures; the guidance of British emigrants to British colonies; and the revision of the Passengers Act of 1855, in accordance with the intentions of its framers, are measures which will increase our trade, knit our Colonies more closely to the mother country, arrest the increase of the dangerous classes, by reducing the supply of competitors for unskilled work in the large towns, and thus contribute to the solution of the terrible social question which, looked at in the mass, is the dismay of statesmen and the despair of philanthropists.

CHAPTER V.

COLONIZATION.

The distinction between emigration and colonization is not generally appreciated by the public. Some of the ex-Colonial Secretaries now living have not mastered the distinction. Emigration is a lonely and hazardous contrivance for the betterment of the individual, by taking passage to another country, and there permeating or being permeated by the influences found on the spot. The depopulation of Ireland between the years 1846 and 1881 was effected by emigration. Colonization is the transfer of an organized community from an old to a new country. The swarming of bees offers the nearest approach to an exact analogy of colonization. Men of Elizabeth's time understood the conditions, and dared the dangers, of successful colonization more perfectly than they are understood in the reign of Her present Majesty. Colonization is a complex and costly process, shrouded with physical, administrative, and political difficulties. It is therefore less popular than emigration as understood by philanthropists, where the payment of passage money begins and ends the work to be done. Colonization begins where emigration leaves off. The circumstances under which a scheme of colonization may be conducted to a successful issue in the present era are worth examination.

In the first place it is well to understand that there are but two spots on the earth's surface available for colonization, subject to the control of the English Cabinet. These territories are Bechuanaland and Western Australia. The surrender of all the Crown lands in all the other British Colonies, to the descendants of the first white settlers, necessitates negotiation with the Governments of those white settlers before the necessary land can be acquired otherwise than by purchase. The Governments of the Anglo-Saxon Colonies are elected and maintained in power by wage-earners; and the electorate naturally regard with abhorrence any measures likely to reduce the rate of wages or to lengthen the hours of work. In South Africa, for example, the Government of the Cape Colony has at its disposal eighteen million acres of good and bad land, but the conservatism of the Dutch and Africander element of the population extinguishes any germinal enthusiasm lurking in the minds of the Cape Ministry for well-considered schemes of colonization. The first impediment to organized colonization, therefore, is the fact that either the colony must be planted by grace of the Imperial power in one of the two Crown Colonies situated in temperate climates, or the land for settlement must be obtained *by purchase* from private holders or the Colonial Governments themselves.

Assuming that the land has been obtained, that it enjoys an adequate rainfall, is well watered, adapted for the cultivation of garden stuff, as well as for the growth of cereals and the maintenance of stock; the pioneer work of surveying and dividing the land into allotments, erecting temporary dwellings, providing stores, furniture, bedding, waggons, carts, cattle, sheep, seed, agricultural implements, and the hundred other necessaries of agricultural existence must be undertaken and completed in advance of the arrival of the main body of settlers on the land. Rations for six months must be laid in and issued, pending the production of food on the spot.

The selection of settlers, more especially in a pioneer undertaking, is a matter of paramount importance. No one should be included who has previously visited and returned from the Colonies. Settlers should be married, as otherwise the men will become nomadic and possibly vicious in their habits; they should not be more than thirty-five years of age, and not encumbered with more than two children apiece. Practical knowledge of agricultural work, temperate habits, and good character are essential. To ensure against one of the commonest causes of failure the exclusion of drink from a new settlement may be regarded as an indispensable precaution. There may be no desire to impose an ascetic habit of life by insisting on abstinence, but experience shows that the prospects of success in a new colony are greatly increased if the drink is resolutely and altogether excluded.

Agricultural labourers should form the bulk of the pioneer parties of settlers in a new colony. Two carpenters, blacksmiths, masons, and handy men for every hundred settlers may advantageously be included; but in no case should these artizans be chosen from large towns. The excitement of a great city indisposes the townsman to the monotonous toil of frontier life, while his *physique* is generally wanting in the toughness necessary to success. It cannot be urged that the selection of an agricultural community is no solution of one of the problems of a great city. It is from the crowds now pouring into the towns from country districts that choice may be made. Farm labourers out of employment are either potential townsmen or potential settlers. Facilities offered to enable them to become settlers and not townsmen, are in effect a direct solution of one factor in the overcrowding problem, since the diversion of the stream of labour from where it is a source of disaster to places where it is a source of wealth, both directly and indirectly, is as beneficial to the great cities as to the colonist himself, or to the colony of which he becomes a part.

The government and administration of justice in a self-contained colony is a matter requiring careful consideration. Subject to the general laws prevailing in the country in which the settlement is placed, disputes arising between settler and settler are better settled on the spot than by recourse to litigation and the arbitrament of the magistrate.

In the *Mir* of the Russian villages, or the *Gansabawa* of Indian and Sinhalese rural communities, we have types of a Village Council suitable to a simple, but orderly system of society. The election of three village elders by the settlers themselves for every hundred members of the community, whose decisions shall be binding in all such matters remitted to them as do not conflict with the jurisdiction of the general law, will be found in practice to be an effectual method of maintaining the peace of the community. The Village Council so chosen will also be fitted to deal with all matters of communal interest, such as commonage rights : the sequence in the use of agricultural implements or machinery common to the settlement : education : and other matters relating to the welfare of the commonwealth. The meetings of the Council should take place weekly. For this purpose a meeting-place should be provided, which will also serve as church-house, schoolroom, and general place of assembly. Elections to the Village Council should take place yearly.

Failures in schemes of colonization are not infrequently the result of ignorance of local conditions, usages, and customs. Administration from London of the details of a new settlement over the sea is a hopeless task, and one which, if attempted, is predestined to failure. Essential, therefore, and a primary condition of success, is the presence on the spot of an old colonist or colonists who will undertake the responsible task of organizing all the details for the selection of land, survey of the allotments, and preparation for the reception of emigrants. It is better to have a Committee of old colonists than to depend on the judgment of an individual, as the wisdom of numbers is apparent in counsel. The real labours of the organization of a successful colony devolve on this Committee, and where their labours are followed by success, the honours which are too often lavished by England on participation in the operations of war, or of State ceremonial, may well be conferred on those who have organized victory from the stubborn elements with which they have to deal.

The relations of the settlers to the Committee should be laid down with exactness before leaving England. The following agreement is the production of experienced colonists, and is actually employed in one such settlement as that described in this chapter.

Conditions of Emigration under ———— Colonization Scheme.

I. Each family will have from 20 to 50 acres for agricultural purposes and homestead, as well as the use of a certain amount of land for communal grazing.

II. Each occupant will have absolute possession of his section of land, and will be entitled to graze on the common-land, ten head of cattle and ten sheep, each head of cattle to represent four sheep; thus, should he prefer to keep sheep only, he would have the right to graze fifty.

III. Each family will be provided on arrival with temporary house accommodation, consisting of two good-sized huts, and necessary household furniture will be provided.

IV. Each section will be accurately surveyed, for the prevention of disputes as to boundaries, etc.

V. Sufficient cattle, ploughs, seed, waggons, or Scotch carts, &c., will, at the discretion of the Local Committee, be supplied to enable the emigrants to get a fair start in working the land, but two or more families will have to participate jointly in the use of the same when required by the Committee.

VI. Provisions will be served out to each family for the first six months if required.

VII. No charge will be made for the first year either for passage-money, rent, interest, rates, or taxes; from which date forward a rental will be charged of £10 per annum, exclusive of rates and taxes, per family, payable half-yearly, to cover interest and wear and tear. Should it be necessary to make any advance in individual cases, the Committee at its discretion will do so, charging interest for such at the rate of five per cent. per annum.

VIII. The cost of each allotment of land, with grazing rights as hereinbefore mentioned, together with the expenses of locating each emigrant family, is estimated to average about £200 sterling.

IX. The holding and stock to become the property of the tenant on payment of the amount of such cost and expenses, and any payments made on account shall bear five per cent. interest. Should any tenant desire to dispose of his land and stock, the consent of the Committee thereto must be first obtained and purchaser approved. The Committee, however, in all cases to have the first option of purchase, the tenant being entitled to any amount realized over and above the sum due to the Committee.

X. Any emigrant convicted of any serious crime, or who fails faithfully to fulfil his obligations under these conditions, or is found drunk and disorderly, will be liable to be ejected from his holding summarily by the Committee, who will at once, and without process of law, resume possession of all property delivered to such emigrant.

XI. In case of such ejectment, the Committee will give the emigrant credit for the value of any improvements made by him on his holding and for any sums of money received from him; and should the total amount of the same exceed the amount in which such emigrant is indebted on account of the expenses aforesaid, including any special advance which may have been made to him by the Committee, the balance in favour of the emigrant shall be paid to him by the Committee.

XII. Facilities for educational purposes will be provided, information regarding which will be detailed in due course.

XIII. Emigrants will embark in London,

and disembark at ———, in the Colony of ———. They will then proceed to their destination in ———.

I, the undersigned, ———, do hereby agree to the aforegoing conditions of emigration, and I do further covenant and promise faithfully to perform all the obligations by the said conditions imposed upon me.

Given under my hand at ———, this ——— day of ———, 188—.

The first principle guiding the administration of a new settlement must be non-shrinkage of capital. If capital is lost, alms have been bestowed which might as well have been thrown in the sea. Repayment by the settlers of their advances is only possible when the settlers themselves are capable and efficient. Efficiency, therefore, must be rigidly prescribed in the choice of settlers, and a resolute maintenance of the highest standard is the truest kindness both to those who leave the mother country and to those who remain behind.

Ambitious projects involving the expenditure of hundreds of thousands, and even of millions of money, are from time to time submitted to the consideration of the Colonial Office. Paper security is all that can be offered as a pledge of the return of the capital advanced, and consequently no ambitious scheme on a large scale has yet received the support of a responsible Minister. From study and experience I am of opinion that success is more likely to attend the organization of small colonizing schemes than those of more ambitious proportions. For the sum of ten thousand pounds from three to four hundred souls can be planted out with every reasonable prospect of a return of the capital invested. Much tact, industry, and skill are required in the organization of a new settlement; but in no department of enterprise is the result of success so rich and so permanent as in the establishment of a new colony. Exactly three hundred years have elapsed since the enterprising navigators of Elizabeth's reign planted the first English Colony in Virginia. Gilbert and Raleigh contended with difficulties to which this generation is a stranger. To-day the task is easier, but no less fraught with the destinies of a great nation. Gilberts and Raleighs are still to be found capable and wise enough to conduct to a successful issue colonizing schemes appropriate to our changed conditions of life. Ecclesiastical tyranny no longer drives into the wilderness legions of Huguenots or of Puritans. But the pressure of want ever tightening its grip over masses of the population supplies all the centrifugal force formerly generated by the cruelty of priests and the persecutions of bigot kings.

Colonization in the nineteenth century has been suspended. It is the one problem which requires money to set it in action and to conduct the process of settlement to a final issue. Much of the money expended in emotional charities, and in the maintenance of paid secretaries, might as well be poured into the sea for all the permanent good effected by the expenditure. Divert the stream of pauper-raising charities to supporting a system of colonization, and the public will have, at all events, some assurance of permanently (and without the waste or extinction of capital) converting idle labourers into producers of wealth for themselves and for those left at home, with whom rivalry for a crust will have ceased for ever.

CHAPTER VI.

OVERCROWDING.

THE magnetism of large cities is characterised as much by the intensity as by the volume of evil generated within the field of influence. The effects on the health and character of the working classes, resulting from overcrowding, are numerous; it is a plague-spot of furious vitality: so prolific of disease to body and mind, that the stream of philanthropy has exhausted effort in wetting a sore when it should cleanse a cancer, and in dealing with effects when fully developed, instead of drowning them in the centre at their birth. Overcrowding is a central evil round which the others are grouped. The unit of the problem of overcrowding is the one-room system. The result of the one-room system is the one-bed system, and the effect of the one-bed system is somewhat to mitigate the advantages of the system of national education, on the subject of which the English people are so cock-a-whoop. The single-room system forges incest, illegitimacy, juvenile prostitution, drunkenness, dirt, idleness, disease, and a death-rate higher than that of Grosvenor Square. The rate of mortality in a certain quarter of St. Pancras was stated by Dr. Murphy to have reached in 1882 the enormous rate of 70·1 per thousand. The average death-rate for England is 19·6 per thousand. Much suffering is caused to little children in overcrowded districts, which does not appear in the death-rate. Their happiness is impaired and their health injured by breathing air tainted by disease. In St. Luke's, ophthalmia, locally known as the blight, is prevalent. Scrofula and congenital diseases are also prevalent among the young children. Typhus is intimately connected with overcrowding; but infectious and even fatal disease is not so great an evil as the general reduction of stamina all round resulting from the generic poison of overcrowded centres.

On the authority of the Royal Commission on the Housing of the Working Classes (1885), the evils of overcrowding are a "public scandal," and are becoming, in certain localities, " more serious than they ever were." Much legislation is in existence, designed to meet these evils, but the atrocious want of system, the character of some of those to whom the administration of local government is entrusted, added to the idle game indulged in by the House of Commons, known as " permissive legislation," combine to increase the output of evils of which all are aware.

The existing legislation on the subject is as follows :—

In 1851 Lord Shaftesbury carried the Common Lodging Houses Act and the Labouring Classes Lodging Houses Act.

In 1885 the Nuisances Removal Act was carried by Sir Benjamin Hall.

In 1868 Mr. Torrens, Mr. Locke, and Mr. Kinnaird obtained legislation, after two years' debates, conversations, cross-examinations, rejoinders, inquiries, and investigations, which dealt with the provision of " better dwellings for artizans and labourers."

In 1875, 1879, and 1882 the Artizans' Dwellings Improvements Acts, commonly known as "Cross's Act," became law.

In 1881-1882 Select Committees of the House of Commons were appointed to consider the working of the Torrens' and Cross's Acts. The Reports of these Committees were followed by Mr. Shaw Lefevre's Artizans' Dwellings Act, 1882.

Despite the wisdom and expert knowledge of which this clotted mass of legislation is the monument, the evils attacked by the Governments of the last thirty years " have not only continued, but have in some places increased in the most aggravated manner " (Report of Royal Commission). The will of Parliament has been exerted perfunctorily. Sussex and Argyleshire are indifferent to Stepney and Bethnal Green. East London has hitherto never been articulate, and thus evils which would frenzy the nation were they to happen in Fort Qu'appelle or Cawnpore are accepted with languid remorse by the country at large.

Gross neglect and corruption by members of the local Vestries and Boards of Guardians contribute largely to the state of affairs in

East London. The work, for example, of house drainage is imperfectly done—largely in consequence of there being little supervision on the part of the local authorities. Bad sanitary arrangements usual in the poor man's house are incredible to the comfortable classes. Ashpits and dustbins are few and far between. Refuse vegetable matter is thrown into open dustholes, and poisons in the process of decomposition the air of close courts. The neglect by the local authority of dustbins is the means of communicating scarlet fever to whole rows of houses. In the metropolis the law provides:—

"First, that the vestry or district board, as the case may be, must—(*a*) appoint and employ persons; or (*b*) contract with some company or persons for collecting and removing all dirt, ashes, rubbish, and filth in houses and places within their parish or district. The scavengers so employed or contracted with, or their servants, are to perform their duties on such days, and at such hours, and in such manner as the vestry or district board from time to time appoint. The penalty for neglect of duty on the part of the scavenger is a sum not exceeding £5 for every offence (18 and 19 Vict., c. 120, s. 125). An occupier or person who refuses or does not permit any soil, dirt, ashes, or filth to be taken away by the scavengers, or who obstructs the scavengers in the performance of their duty, is liable for every offence to a penalty not exceeding £5 (18 and 19 Vict., c. 120, s. 126).

"Second, as to urban sanitary districts, *i.e.*, boroughs, Local Government districts, and Improvement Act districts—Every urban sanitary authority may, and when required by order of the Local Government Board, must, undertake or contract for—(*a*) the removal of house refuse from premises ; (*b*) the cleansing of ashpits, either for the whole or any part of the district. If any person removes, or obstructs the authority or contractor in removing, any of the matters above mentioned which are authorized to be removed by the authority, he is liable for the offence to a penalty not exceeding £5 (38 and 39 Vict., c. 55, s. 42). If the authority, who have themselves undertaken or contracted for the removal of house refuse from premises, or the cleansing of ashpits, fail, without reasonable excuse, after notice in writing, from the occupier of any house within their district, requiring them to remove any house refuse, or to cleanse any ashpit belonging to the house, or used by the occupiers of it, to cause the same to be removed or cleansed, as the case may be, within seven days, the authority will be liable to pay to the occupier of the house a penalty not exceeding 5s. for every day during which the default continues after the expiration of the period of seven days (38 and 39 Vict., c. 55, s. 43). But where the sanitary authority do not themselves undertake or contract for—(*a*) the removal of house refuse ; (*b*) the cleansing of ashpits belonging to any premises ; they may make bye-laws imposing the duty of cleansing or removal, at such intervals as they think fit, upon the occupier of the premises.

" The sanitary authority may also make bye-laws for the prevention of nuisances arising from filth, dust, ashes, and rubbish (38 and 39 Vict., c. 55, s. 44). The authority may provide in proper and convenient situations receptacles for the temporary deposit and collection of dust, ashes, and rubbish; and they may also provide fit buildings and places for the deposit of the matters collected by them (38 and 39 Vict., c. 55, s. 45).

" Although this is not the place for the consideration of matters connected with rural sanitary districts, it may be mentioned that the provisions in force are the same as in urban sanitary districts, except those set out in the last paragraph above."—(Report of the Royal Commission on the Housing of the Working Classes, p. 9.)

The water supply in the poorer portions of London is inadequate, and the source of misery, and unhealthiness and misery. Personal cleanliness, the mark of a gentle mind, is impossible where the supply of water is uncertain, and where, from the absence of storage accommodation, it has to be kept in tubs, and often in the foul atmosphere of sleeping-rooms. Even when there is a supply in the houses, they are often supplied from one and the same cistern, for the purpose of flushing the sanitary arrangements and quenching the thirst. The cistern is often uncovered, and close to the closet pan and the dust heap.

Much power is confided to the local authorities in regard to the provision of closet accommodation. In Clerkenwell, cases occur of one closet for sixteen houses. Indigent Italians engaged in the ice-cream and barrel-organ trade have peculiarly offensive habits. Remissness of the local authorities, and the nebulous state of the law on the question as to the difference between a servant and a lodger, combine to produce a condition of things which had better be left to the imagination.

Offensive trades carried on in insanitary dwellings give rise to peculiarly energetic, capable, and efficient germs of disease. Rags saturated with filth, picked in unventilated rooms, are the vehicles of virulent fevers and contagious disorders. Such trades, such as matchbox making, requiring the use of paste, especially in warm weather, are especially disgusting. Rabbit-pulling is, perhaps, the most pernicious, as the air is charged with fluff; and when a stray sunbeam shoots athwart the murky room, the atmosphere appears solid enough to be sliced with a bread-knife. Fish are cured and smoked in bedrooms inhabited by human beings, and the costermonger restores his haddocks, watercresses, and fruit—which have been deposited beneath his bed for the night—by anointing them with the water which has been described by Canon Farrar as "the pure diamond of God."

The absence of a general system of mortuaries involves the retention in the living-room of the family of a corpse until the funeral takes place. In the interval between the death and interment the ordinary habits of life are maintained. Eating, drinking, and sleeping in the company of the dead is gruesome to the mind; and when the body remains unburied for a lengthened period—as is usual among the poor—the health of the living is endangered, if not impaired.

As mortuaries are rare, and, under the present form of local government, are unlikely to increase, the only remedy for this evil is the enactment of a measure providing for the burial of corpses within forty-eight hours of death. The customary delay which is allowed to elapse in England between death and burial, especially among the poorer classes, has no parallel in other civilized countries. The custom is attended by no advantage, and it is difficult to discover any reasons why this period should not at all events be materially curtailed.

Overcrowding is partly due to the structural defects of houses built for other purposes, but inhabited from cellar to garret by the poorest folk. Houses built for the well-to-do merchant of George the Second's time have passed through many vicissitudes before arriving at the tenement period of their existence, when they become the object of well-meaning, but ineffectual legislation. Nominal owners have parted with effectual control, and the inevitable consequence is the disregard of all the intermediate profit-mongers for the condition in which tenement property is kept. No radical improvement in the housing of the poor can take place until the principle is accepted by the Legislature that no original owner can by sub-letting alienate responsibility where he continues to receive profit. The necessary misery of many as essential to the profit of one is conformable neither to the Sermon on the Mount nor to the enactments of just law. Nothing short of the expropriation of defaulting owners and the suppression of the present form of local government will meet the difficulty; and, in any case, the indignation of the public at the perpetuation of remediable evils for the sake of gain, when men's lives are the counters, must be aroused against the evil-doers.

Among the well-to-do an eighth to a tenth of the income is spent in rent. Among the poor, according to Mr. Marchant Williams, Inspector of Schools for the London School Board, eighty-eight per cent. of the dwellers in certain poor quarters of London spend more than one-fifth of their income in rent; forty-six per cent. pay from one-fourth to one-half; forty-two per cent. pay from one-fourth to one-fifth; and only twelve per cent. pay less than one-fifth of their weekly wages in rent. Four shillings is the average rent of one room, and six shillings of two. The disproportion between rent and wages is increasing in intensity in certain parts of London. Congestion proceeds apace, while wages are not rising; casual labourers and many of the poorer artizans are compelled to live near their work. Workmen's trains are luxuries for a higher rank in society. Dock labourers must be in readiness for a "call," which may arise at any moment. White men in the heart of London are fighting any winter morning, like Esquimaux dogs over a piece of blubber, for the work that only a few can get. Even skilled artizans, such as Clerkenwell watchmakers, not owning all the expensive tools required by their delicate trade, must borrow once or twice a day, and must return the apparatus with punctuality. This prevents their living at a distance from their work. Girls engaged in the artificial flower trade must be in attendance whether there be work for them or not; for, like the Dock hands, if they be not within hail, they lose the chance of casual employment.

The pressure caused by the immigration of foreign Jews, especially into Whitechapel, Spitalfields, and St. George's-in-the-East, is another cause of overcrowding. So serious is this question of the immigration of the indigent foreigner, that some consideration of the subject may not be out of place.

In the United States, British Columbia, and in Australia, the indigent foreigner of the Mongolian variety has received the earnest attention of the Legislatures concerned. While it is not urged that the Chinaman and the indigent German Jew are in all respects similar, there is sufficient identity in the two problems to render an examination into the merits of the Chinese Exclusion Acts interesting and important.

The case for the exclusion of Chinese from the English Colonies is as follows:—

1. That they arrive in the country faster than any other kind of immigrant.

2. That they are superior in number to our own race.

3. That they are not disposed to be governed by our laws.

4. That they are dissimilar in habits and occupation to our own people.

5. That they evade the payment of taxes justly due to the Government.

6. That they are governed by pestilential habits.

7. That they are useless in cases of emergency.

8. That they habitually desecrate graveyards by the removal of bodies therefrom.

9. That the laws governing the whites are found to be inapplicable to Chinese.

10. That they are inclined to habits subversive of the comfort and well-being of the community.

Certain of the charges in this indictment are unjust if sought to be applied to the indigent foreigner, who contributes so largely to the overcrowding problem of our great cities. Some of the counts are only too true; and so bitterly is the justice of these charges felt by those suffering from the immigration, it would not be surprising to witness a *jüdenhasse* in the heart of London. Temperate in their habits, and with a low standard of comfort, the poor foreigner evades all taxation in England, while he presses heavily on the poorer English in the struggle for existence. While the United States, with all her boasted freedom, relentlessly rejects and returns on our hands all indigent English or Irish emigrants who knock at the door of the Immigrant Depôt at Castle Garden—England, the home of cant as well as of the free, admits, without a protest, all the poor souls driven from Silesian soil by the imperious necessities of Bismarckian policy. Germany is a great country, and Bismarck is an eminent man; but why England should remain content to act as rubbish-heap to the great country and the eminent man, when neither America nor our own Colonies will take a single pauper from us, passes all understanding. This remonstrance is no political indictment, and appeals to neither party nor passion. England will cease to be England if our rulers do not show that they love the English more than the frugal, unlovable foreigner. Cant and hypocrisy may talk of freedom and England being a sanctuary for the desolate and oppressed. Freedom to starve and to go to the streets for Englishmen and English girls, is to be set against the vicarious hospitality quidnuncs would continue to extend to indigent foreigners, and thus constrain their unwilling companions and rivals of English blood, by the riotous excesses of political economy, to seek a sanctuary in starvation, and repose in death. So long as the evil was restricted, the hospitality and the freedom of England were topics well calculated to regale the national appetite for sentiment and ideas. Now that the evil is growing apace, and becomes apparent even to those who are not crowded out of existence by the competition of untaxed strangers within our gates, the question arises as to what is the best method of grappling with the difficulty.

Public opinion in England is not sufficiently robust to reject, at the port of disembarkation, paupers of foreign blood ; and, owing to local circumstances, any inquiry instituted on landing into the means of the immigrant would easily be baffled or evaded. The only remedy apparent to me is the imposition of a poll-tax, which should not be less in amount than eight pounds. It could be made recoverable from employers in the same manner as income tax is collected from public companies on behalf of their *employés*. If it be objected that Germany and other States will retaliate by the imposition of similar taxation, the obvious reply is that settlement in our own Colonies will receive a stimulus, and national development will thus be concentrated within the circumference of the empire.

The magnetic attraction exerted by the mass of a great city on the impressionable minds of agricultural labourers who are driven from the soil is in itself one overwhelming cause of the overcrowding problem. Nevertheless, artificial encouragement is given to the increase of population by the advertisements of contractors for provincial labour when labour in excess is present on the spot. The extension of the Metropolitan and District Railways was carried out by bringing up people from the provinces when men in plenty were obtainable on the spot. Contractors do not regard city labourers with favour. Industry and sobriety are found more usually in the rural than in the urban population. The Rev. R. C. Billing, a clergyman with great knowledge of the subject, considers that, if it could be done, some attempt should be made to counteract those proceedings of advertising to bring labour to an over-stocked market. It is probable that any such attempt, to be practicable, must take the form of improving the moral and physical status of the poorer inhabitants of a great city, rather than that of legislative interference with the execution of contract works.

Immigration with all its evils, and from whatever cause, is not so serious a factor in the overcrowding problem as demolitions and the consequent displacement of population. Demolitions may be divided into five classes.

1. Clearances undertaken by owners for the improvement of their property when no provision is made for the poor tenants.

2. Clearances effected by the local authority under statutory powers for the erection of artizans' dwellings in the place of the buildings demolished.

3. Demolitions for the widening and improvement of public streets.

4. Demolitions undertaken in consequence of the erection of public buildings.

5. Demolitions carried out by Railway Companies for the enlargement and construction of their termini, lines, and stations.

The first of these classes presents, in an extreme form, the logical issue of the rights of property; one where an intellectual assent to the exercise of such rights is demanded from people who are incapable of according their assent. As a wild blackbird cannot resist black currants growing in a garden, so men, evicted for another's gain, with no covert in which to lay their head, cannot resist the conclusion that the laws of life are superior to the laws of property; and that political economy is subordinate to the higher laws of humanity and justice. Those whose need is greatest suffer most acutely.

The second class of demolition is undertaken from humane motives, but is the cause of hardship from the manner in which the arrangements are carried out. Rents are raised in adjacent districts, and it happens sometimes that the poor are turned out of fairly well-ordered rooms, and are compelled to make their new abode in quarters several degrees lower in quality, and not lower in rental.

Next come the street improvements. Perhaps this is the worst of all the classes, for the poor, often ejected only by the sound of the pick and crowbar at their very threshold, overcrowd the surrounding neighbourhood, send up rents, and often " sink into a miserable mode of life, after being accustomed to decency and cleanliness."

Sites for the erection of School Boards are necessarily chosen in the most crowded parts of the town, and consequently occasion distress similar in character to that arising from public improvements.

The inability of the poor to protect themselves is rarely more conspicuous than when receiving notices to remove from their dwellings by the agents of a Railway Company. They do not appreciate the fact until the roof is about their ears. As in Calcutta, the British Government appoint a Protector of Emigrants for the benefit of those natives who contemplate a sojourn on the plantations of the Mauritius or the West India Islands, so in London an Imperial Protector of Residents is needed for the guardianship of those inhabitants of the human warrens, who share with the rabbit the characteristics of timidity, suspicion, and fecundity.

At the present time Inspectors of Nuisances are appointed by vestries and district boards, and are subordinate to the worthies who adorn these distinguished assemblies. There are not many of these Inspectors, and they have so much to do their existence cannot be regarded as offering a serious contribution to the overcrowding problem. In Islington there is one Inspector to fifty-six thousand inhabitants. Eighty-six thousand inhabitants of Bermondsey divide between them a whole Inspector. St. James's, Westminster, has one Inspector to every nine thousand population, but on this vestry—according to the Report of the Royal Commission—were "thirteen or fourteen persons who are interested in bad and doubtful property." Sanitary Inspectors whose office and pay are subject to the pleasure of such a body may be expected to be supine. Clerkenwell basks in the sunshine of notoriety both from the state of the homes of the working classes, and from the remarkable characteristics of some members of the assembly administering its local affairs.

As an example of the class of appointment made by the local authorities of some portions of London, the evidence of Mr. Robert Paget, Clerk to the Vestry of Clerkenwell, reveals some singular practices. It appears from this gentleman's evidence before the Royal Commission (Q. 17,679) that one of the sanitary inspectors of the parish acts also as sexton, coroner's officer, messenger to the vestry, and that the training enjoyed by this versatile functionary to fit him for the charge of the lives and health of thousands of human beings was that "he was something in the jewellery trade." It is clear from such an instance as this that, pending changes in the government of London, the Local Government Board should be entrusted with a veto on the appointment of parochial sanitary officials.

The truth must be told, and it cannot be refuted. Vestrymen, voracious, incapable, devoid of public spirit, swarm like locusts on a field of young millet, fatten on the ratepayers, taint the record of public life, check the resolves of humane officials, and betray the interests they are elected to protect. Saturated with corruption, and incompetent, the present form of Local Government in London is doomed. Counterfeit representation leads to illusory forms of protecting the poor and needy—forms which are but phantoms flitting to and fro, powerless to right great wrongs, or to carry out the permanent, solid, and straightforward purposes of an honest and hearty desire to attenuate evil and advance the good.

Forty-five acres of land are available in London on the removal of the prisons for the erection of artizans' dwellings.

The Public Prosecutor should, as the only functionary competent to do so, proceed against owners or holders of insanitary property on behalf of those who have suffered injury or loss to property or health. To invest an impoverished apple-woman with the power of bringing a civil action against the Duke of Westminster or his middlemen and sub-lessees is one of those legislative quips of which the Adulteration Act presents another conspicuous example.

The recommendations of the main body of the Royal Commissioners partake of a temporising character. It is necessary to clear away root and branch the present vestry system. No legislation designed to impress on the local authority a sense of their duty in relation to the vigorous enforcement of sanitary laws can be efficacious when no sense of duty finds a place in the consciences and the hearts of many of those who are typical representatives of the present system. A Municipality for London conceived on Imperial lines, with a system of representation sufficiently wide in scope to evoke the patriotic services of worthy citizens, is of the first necessity if measures are seriously undertaken with the object of bettering the condition of the poor. Water supply, sanitary accommodation, responsibility of owners, abatement of nuisances, are details of great moment, but subordinate in importance to the greater question of providing administrative machinery adequate to grapple with the tremendous problem with which it has to deal, and manned by men enjoying the confidence of the public.

CHAPTER VII.

ADULTERATION.

Mahomet, at the Farewell pilgrimage, enjoined his followers in these words :—

"And your slaves! see that ye feed them with such food as ye eat yourselves, and clothe them with the same stuff ye wear. And if they commit a fault which ye incline not to forgive, then sell them; for they are the servants of the Lord, and are not to be tormented."

The white serfs of capital are tormented with many evils. Not the least of these evils is the tainted food and drink supplied to them under the present system. Mr. Bright is in a measure responsible for the palsy that has stayed the hand of the law and shaken the opinion of the public in regard to the matter of adulteration. It is a "form of competition," says the right honourable Gentleman. That little phrase has had wide and far-reaching effects in composing the consciences of venal traders. "It is a form of competition," whispers the grocer to himself, as he sands his sugar or waters his vinegar. Food and drink are persistently debased by spurious ingredients; quality is counterfeited, bulk increased, appearance improved, and constituents abstracted with impunity. Legislation does not lag. It is not enforced. The Act of 1872 is an excellent measure—for well-to-do people. The proof of its excellence is shown by the quality of the tea and sugar well-to-do people are able to buy. When the poor man buys his two-pennyworth of "coffee," half-ripe, insect-eaten and sea-damaged, blended with chicory which has been treated to an admixture of beans, acorn flour, lupin seed, "Hambro' powder," mangold wurtzel, and spent tan, the law says to him—"If you have reason to believe your purchase is adulterated, you can set in motion the machinery of the Sale of Foods Act by placing a deposit varying from half-a-crown to half-a-guinea in the hands of the local authority. If, on analysis, your suspicions are confirmed by the scientific gentlemen with competent medical, chemical, and microscopical knowledge, your deposit shall be returned to you." The poor man, however, does not happen to have a spare half-guinea available for scientific research, and he is unacquainted with the existence of the beneficent legislation which has been enacted for his behoof. As a natural consequence, the Adulteration Act of 1875 is essentially a piece of class legislation. It is adapted to protect the rich man and his family. To the care of the venal and voracious vestrymen is left the protection of the tribe of poor. Tea in the East End is remarkable for characteristics acquired after being despatched from Canton or Calcutta. Floor dust and sweepings are the principal ingredients.

Bread is adulterated with rice. In practice 100 lbs. of flour will make from 133 lbs. to 137 lbs. of bread; so that a sack of 280 lbs. of flour should yield 95 four-pound loaves. The baker's skill is shown by contriving to increase the number. This he effects by the addition of a gummy mess of boiled rice, which enables him to increase his out-turn by five per cent. Such bread generates obscure fungoids with rapidity, and on a warm day turns sour in twelve hours.

The test for good flour is its sweetness and freedom from acidity and musty flavour. Good flour, when kneaded, yields a tough, elastic gluten, which, when baked in an oven, expands and appears of a rich brown colour. Bad flour makes a ropy-looking gluten, difficult of manipulation, and is of a dirty brown colour when baked. Oils are adulterated with inferior kinds, and the fraud is detected by means of the specific gravity of the oils.

Isinglass is adulterated with gelatine, the fraud being so contrived as to retain, to some extent, the well-known character of genuine isinglass. The true isinglass may be recognised from the false in the following way: immersed in cold water the shreds of genuine isinglass become white and opaque like cotton threads, and they swell equally in all directions, whereas those of gelatine become transparent and ribbon-like.

Mustard is so powerful in flavour it is commonly diluted with flour, turmeric being added to improve the appearance. Genuine mustard does not contain starch, and does not become blue when treated with a solution of iodine.

The bees of English cottagers flit from flower to flower without result, for the adulteration of honey is so universal that there is little or no demand for the genuine English article.

Pepper, cinnamon, curry-powder, ginger, and cayenne are also the subjects of fraudulent adulteration. Linseed meal and powdered capsicums are used for adulterating pepper. Ginger powder is sophisticated with sago, meal rice, and turmeric, while the colouring agents of curry-powder and cayenne are earth, brick-dust, red lead, and vermilion. Spices are sometimes deprived of their active properties before they are ground and sold to the poor.

Beer is adulterated, especially on Saturdays in the small beershops, to give fictitious strength, to improve the body and flavour, and to impart a bitterness. For these purposes tobacco, opium, *indicus cocculus,* capsicums, ground ginger, liquorice, treacle, salt, quassia, gentian, and horehound are employed as adulterants. The brutal violence so often committed after an orgie on beer only is probably caused by the maddening influences of some of these ingredients. It is needless to describe the adulterants employed in degrading the qualities of wines at Hamburg and elsewhere, as wine is not consumed in the East End—except on high days and holidays, when some bacchanalian may call for a "pot of port" to treat his boon companions.

The adulteration of spirits consists mostly in the use of raw and inferior spirit. The *newness* of spirit is a great evil. East-Enders have acquired a taste for fusel oil. Ripe old whisky, ten years old, drunk in equal quantities, would probably impart a tone of sobriety to the densely-populated quarters of which we are speaking.

Butter is probably seldom sold to the very poor. One shilling a pound is the price of the grease sold to them as butter. Fat and mud appear to be the constituents employed in this department of dairy industry. Milk is adulterated with the adulterated water sold by the water companies. The same "form of competition" enters into the preparation of sugar, which contains insoluble ingredients—flour, oatmeal, and arrowroot.

Meat is adulterated, under the meaning of the Act, by selling as English that which is really of American or Australasian origin. Twenty-five million pounds of frozen mutton are annually imported into England. Most of this meat is fraudulently sold as English mutton. Until a master butcher is tied down over an ants' nest, or otherwise visited with the displeasure of society, the practice of falsifying the character of meat is likely to continue. What is known as "croaker" meat (Scottish *braxie*)—flesh from an animal dying a natural death—is disposed of by costermongers. Inspectors of Nuisances now and then prosecute the salesmen of this bad meat, and sometimes a conviction ensues. Pickles are in much favour in the East End, and from the admixture of copper do not escape the universal contamination. Relishes such as bright green pickles are used to season the digestion of offal purchased of "cag-mag" butchers. Savouries are much liked.

Adulteration in other countries is strictly

prohibited under penal obligations. The Prussian penal code provides that any person selling adulterated or spoiled goods shall be fined, or, as an alternative, imprisoned for six weeks, with confiscation of goods; and it is not necessary to prove that the seller was aware of the adulteration. In Holland, and in France by the Code Napoléon, a sentence of imprisonment varying from six days to two years may be inflicted.

The manner in which the materials for food and drink are adulterated in England is exemplified by a little story. There were three flies who were great friends. These flies started on a journey in search of something to eat. They came to a piece of bread; one of the flies being very hungry stepped in advance of his companions and fastened eagerly on to the bread; it contained alum, and the fly died in great agony from the contraction of his digestive apparatus. His remaining companions, oppressed with grief, mourned his loss, but hunger compelled them to seek subsistence. They arrived at a bowl of sugar, of which one partook; the sugar contained sulphuric acid, and one more un-

M

happy insect laid down his life. The survivor, bereft of his companions, determined to end by suicide his lonely existence, so he alighted on a fly-paper, partook of the poison thereon, and prepared himself for death, but to his surprise he found that instead of death or disease he had made a good and healthy meal —the fly-paper was adulterated.

No remedy for adulteration of the food and drink of the poor is possible until the present tangle of local government is cut away. To burden East End ratepayers with a large increase to the existing inspectorial staff is impracticable and unjust. The equalization of rates is a measure which must precede any serious effort to grapple with the widespread degradation of food. The next step is to increase the numbers of the Inspectors of Nuisances, and to support those gentlemen in their task by inflicting far more serious punishment on adulterators than is possible under existing legislation. Increased severity in the punishment for this class of offence is justified in the interests of posterity. If public opinion is ripe for the imprisonment of those who are guilty of adulterating bayonets, or supplying unserviceable guns, there is but a short step to be traversed in order to treat as criminal whoever impairs the stamina of the next generation by selling garbage as food, or poison as drink. The evil is national in its dimensions. Nothing short of the exercise of national will can abate and extinguish a system unknown to the heathen, which has already lost to England some of her foreign trade in calicoes and cottons, and which justly exposes her to the contempt and hatred of the simpler and less civilized nations of the earth.

CHAPTER VIII.

DRINK.

As the foot and not the shoemaker is the cause of the shoe, so we must look farther afield for the causes of drunkenness than the present state of the licensing laws. Without the stimulus of legislation the upper classes have become, in two generations, habitually temperate. A sot is no longer regarded by society with the easy temper prevailing at the beginning of the nineteenth century. Prince Bismarck—whose feats with the tankard excite the loving admiration of Busch—speaks of the time when the consumption of strong waters and "huge cups of mixed champagne and porter" were "the indispensable passports into the diplomatic service." Two hundred years ago the chief pleasures of the country gentlemen of England were commonly derived from unrefined sensuality. The quantity of beer consumed in those days was enormous. Beer was then not only all that beer is now, but filled the place, to a large extent, of wine, tea, coffee, chocolate, liqueurs, and ardent spirits. Since the Revolution the drinking habits of the cultivated classes have gradually lessened, until the vice of drunkenness has become the characteristic of the lower and not of the upper stratum of society. Melancholy and monotonous as the lot of the poorest men in a great city must necessarily be, with all the earth but mud and dust paved away from under their feet, and the blue sky always hidden by a canopy of smoke, the imagination is only to be stirred by resort to the stimulus of alcohol, or to the excitements of emotional religion.

Sicilian peasants sing and dance in the intervals of toil under the witchery of sunshine, fruit, and flowers. English labourers of the cities take their pleasure under the stinging impulse of vitriolic intoxicants. Between abstinence and excess there is no middle path. In the submerged stratum of which we are speaking, I am unable to discover the existence of a temperate class, although the abstinent class is larger than is generally supposed. Abstinence and undue indulgence seem to be the only available alternatives. While, therefore, the so-called "Temperance" movement receives great support from the existence of prevailing excess, it has extinguished the moderate class by silencing the moderate men. There is nothing less than an infinite difference in morality and in destiny between a sober and an intemperate man. To confound temperance with total abstinence, which is now the shibboleth of the Temperance Reformers, is to trifle with language, fact, and character. The results of such insincerity are disastrous. Kingsley, who was a man before he was a clergyman, prophesied the consequences of such a Procrustean policy, and the condition of our great cities is witness to the accuracy of his anticipations. Strictly sober men are hustled into shame-faced silence by the innuendoes of abstinent fanatics. What is the result?

Families, schools, churches, trades clubs, who are not taught the doctrine of abstinence, are left untaught on the whole question of alcoholic enjoyment. A population drenched with strong drink, degraded and impoverished beyond the experience of history, are invited to relinquish what is practically their only form of enjoyment, and the invitation is couched in the language of a counsel of perfection. The common people have never responded to the suggestions of heroic self-denial, or to a counsel of perfection, and it is unlikely that the mass of the English people will, in our time, affiliate themselves with the United Kingdom Alliance.

The remedy must be sought elsewhere. In the re-housing of the poor, in the provision of rational entertainments, in the exercise of a more vigilant supervision over the character and purity of the liquors retailed in the public-houses, and in a vigorous reform of the licensing laws may be found material contributions to the solution of one of the greatest of our national problems. The enthusiastic outbreak of *moderate* men in favour of organic changes in the method of grappling with drunkenness is essential to a rational and successful treatment of the temperance question. Too much honour is paid by successive Governments to the drink interests. Beer is coronetted by grateful Ministers; whisky and porter, by the sheer weight of their influence, acquire hereditary distinction without an effort. That Medicine should be without one representative in the House of Lords, while the drink which provides them with most of their patients is crowned with glory and honour, is repugnant to common sense. If we drank ourselves out of the Alabama Claims we have drunk ourselves into a singularly shameful position as a torch-bearer of civilization. We do not hold the torch upright, and we have burnt all the dependent tribes with whom we have come in contact in foreign parts.

American working men, especially the Scandinavians, enjoy their läger beer and are strictly temperate. The absence of a pure and mildly stimulating beverage for habitual use is, perhaps, one of the chief causes of habitual excess in England. If it be unlikely that the whole nation will ever consent to total abstinence, the reasonable course to pursue is to limit the necessary evil, to purify the drink, and to supply other resources for the employment of their time to those who are driven to the low beershop by the sheer necessities and unlovely conditions of their lives.

Public opinion is now so strongly in favour of some form of local option as a means of cutting off the supply and thus reducing the consumption, it is desirable, at all events, to try the experiment, and no more favourable field of operations could be found than those densely populated neighbourhoods which are at once inhabited by the poorest and most degraded of mankind, and dominated by the brewing and publican interests. American experience of local option is by no means conclusive of a successful result ensuing from this class of legislation. Whether the passion for drink be extinguished, or whether it be gratified by stealth, or on the circumference of the prescribed area, is a moot point. On the Shaftesbury Estate in Battersea, where no public-house is allowed to be erected, the inhabitants are remarkable for their freedom from pauperism or crime. On the other hand the circumference of the estate is fringed with public-houses, so that the heart of the district alone is preserved from the temptation presented freely to those dwelling farther from the centre. To draw correct inferences it is necessary that observations should not be based on experiments conducted in too restricted an area. The district chosen should either be compact—that is, square or circular in form—or better still, should include the whole area of a town or city. The results following the closure of disorderly houses in a densely populated parish seem to show that transfer and not extinction of evil is the consequence of action within too limited an area, bordered on all sides by a dense population possessing similar characteristics to that affected by the exclusion of facilities for the sale of drink.

With regard to rivals to the public-house, nothing will succeed in attracting the mass of the people unless it is really entertaining, at all events, in the first instance. Recreation and not instruction is what the poor folk lack. A house for the public where good comic songs, free from the grossness and suggestiveness so common in the public-house "free-and-easy," will draw hundreds, especially if the performers, or some of them, will take personal interest in the cares and welfare of the audience. In a short time, when relations have been established between the hearers and the entertainers, the comic element may be replaced by music of a higher grade. Gradually as intelligence awakes, bright, short lectures on popular topics, easy science, physiology, English history, travels, and biography excite the liveliest interest, and, in a large proportion of cases, lead to the abandonment of the more bestial methods of whiling away of leisure hours. An occasional concert is useless. Open a house for the public, and have some form of excitement provided three or four times a week, and especially on Sunday evenings, and in a short time, and after the exercise of patience and good temper, the people who came to laugh remain to learn. Such houses for the public can be held wherever a large room or small hall is available. They cost but little. A large staff of volunteers is indispensable, since few are willing or able to attend more than once or twice a month. It is to be wished that the churches, chapels, synagogues, school board buildings, and vestry halls were available nightly for the recreation of the people. Dumb churches, buildings in the midst of a brain-soaked population, would seem to be exactly fitted for the real elevation of the habits of the poor. Clerical prejudice, however, for the most part favours the reservation of these buildings for the vocabulary of religion; although the good effects of a constant and prolonged employment of this vocabulary are not traceable in the lives and habits of the great mass of the poorest classes. If you wish to get at the people, you must be, not seem, as they are. It is not necessary to dress or to talk as they do. But the *special* dress and the professional talk of many of the clergy erect impassable barriers between the churches and the drinking people. It is hopeless to expect that a paid professional class can alone carry into effect a revolution in lives and habits which are so largely the results of the neglect by the whole of the community. Each member of society must own to himself or herself the existence of inalienable responsibility which cannot be evaded by a cheque, or discharged by the languid profession of an unpersecuted creed. The drunkenness of great cities is the result of causes for which every comfortable adult is individually and directly responsible. The relentless exertion of the public conscience and the public, and nothing less, will, without fear of labour, or favour of interests, now, even in this decade, mend or end many of the sources of evil which lead to wasting tyranny of habitual excess in intoxicating liquors.

The concentrated expenditure of £100,000 on one spot in the East End for a Palace of Delight, to rival the myriad public-houses, is a dissipation of energy. Poor men cannot afford the practice of riding to their pleasures. Public-houses are prosperous because they are always handy. Fifty small centres of delight would reach a larger public than a central palace, and the money laid out would have gone further. However, the thing is accomplished, and it is to be hoped that the stimulus to providing rational enjoyment to those whose lives are destitute of sunshine and grace may lead to a constant repetition of the noble work carried out by Sir Edmund Currie in so effectual and patriotic a manner.

Drink in the East End is not a local, it is an Imperial question. The passionate longing for excitement, and the longing to escape from the destiny of ugliness and pain, which kills family life in East End homes, is evidence of that rough energy which has dominated weaker races in all parts of the world. We have carried from our great cities a world-girdling influence of appetite and passion. The Indians of America and of Hindostan, the wild races of Australia, the kingly Maories, timid Kanakas, fighting Kaffirs and debased Hottentots, West Coast negroes, effeminate Sinhalese, and the sinewy aborigines of Canada and the North Pacific Coastal islands, have bitter reasons to rue the first day of their encounter with the Anglo-Saxon race. The drinking habits of great cities have permeated the world. Diamond and gold mines, worked with English capital, and carried on under the skilled administration of English engineers, are the baleful centres of waste and death, which cargoes of missionaries neither influence nor destroy. Every man who leaves England is a missionary. He is a standard by which English civilization is gauged. England has been betrayed by her sons abroad. Eight centuries of noble deeds do not atone for the devil's work of one. The simplest ideal of a nation, as of an individual, is, that contact with her shall leave no stain on others. England has not stained; she has polluted with drink and honey-combed with foul disease the lives of those races who still survive a contact all unsought by them. We have done these things, and they cannot be undone. Repentance, if sincere, can only take the form of purging our great cities. St. Boniface wrote to the Archbishop of Canterbury in 800, "I hear that you Saxons are mighty drinkers of ale, and that you are worse than the Jews and heathen about me." It was true, and in a thousand years we have gone from bad to worse. I absolutely disbelieve in the power of law to change habits which are accessible only to the highest moral and intellectual influences. Nevertheless, there are some abuses capable of being arrested by wise legislation. The series of temperance measures passed by the Norwegian Storthing, and known generally as the Gothenburg system, has changed an immoderate into a moderate consumption of alcoholic liquors. This system was tried in the first instance in the smaller towns and villages. At the beginning of 1886, the capital, Christiana, was included among the areas subject to the liquor laws, so great were the results achieved by the trial in smaller areas. The main features of the Gothenburg system are—

1. That alcoholic drinks are dispensed by persons deriving no profit from the sale.

2. That the profits arising from the sale are employed by the local authority towards the expense of local government and the reduction of rates.

3. That food is sold to, and partaken of by customers at the time when drink is purchased.

The genius of the English character would probably resent the last provision; but the transfer of pecuniary interest in sales from the seller to the local authority is a valuable principle, which may be well worth trying when we have a system of local government capable of discharging functions similar to those so successfully carried out by Norwegian Mayors and Counsellors.

It is clear that no diminution of drinking habits can occur without a diminution of drink produced and supplied, and therefore without a reduction of trade profits. Any measures, whether legislative or philanthropic, having for their object the sobriety of the English people, must necessarily be a direct attack on the drink interest. This being so, it is hopeless to expect to evade the hostility of the licensed victuallers, or of the beer barons. Reasonable compensation should be granted for the extinction of *bonâ-fide* interests, since confiscation sanctioned in one department of civil life will not remain content with a single victory. Justice, and nothing more than justice, should be conceded. It will be well to suspend for the present the creation of baronets and peers connected with the drink interests, as however worthy they may be in other respects, the distinctions conferred on those gentlemen are apt to give an erroneous impression to uncivilized heathen races as to the degree of honour in which drink trafficking is held by the better class of Englishmen.

CHAPTER IX.

SOCIALISM.

FRENCH enthusiasts who regard the confinement of Baron Rothschild in the prison of Mazas as the most practical method of placing the social question on a thoroughly sound footing, and of giving to an effete Republic a new lease of life, have many sympathisers on this side of the Straits of Dover. Gesture and passion, no less than the records of modern history, impart to the Socialistic propaganda of the impulsive Gaul a grace that is absent from the burglarious teachings of phlegmatic and half-educated Saxons. English Socialism, nevertheless, under great disadvantages, has made rapid strides since 1880. Mr. Henry George, with the taste for picturesque depravity characteristic of mixed races, from the sand-hills of San Francisco, has excited the land-hunger of English-speaking people in all parts of the world. Poor and almost unknown, a knot of resolute English agitators seized the opportunity arising from the interest excited by the fallacies of the Californian dreamer. They were assisted in their efforts, after one or two abortive attempts, by the imbecile prosecution of an incompetent Minister. Martyrdom, notoriety, power, were conferred at one stroke on the leaders of the Social-Democratic movement by the action of the then Home Secretary: for they obtained without risk, and almost without expense, the brilliant advertisement needed to exploit successfully the elixir of a chemist, or the nostrum of a political demagogue.

The effects of civilization on the poorest classes in great cities, excite the liveliest sympathy of all sorts and conditions of men. The Social-Democratic party arrogate to themselves, however, the virtue of being the only people who have discovered what is wrong, and know what is required to put it right. Socialists conceive their eyes to be endowed with clearer vision than those of other men. For fevers, wastings, palsies befalling all flesh, and entering everywhere, they have a specific; and, as the large majority of the Socialist body entertain no hope of a life to come, the grim ending of sad lives oppresses them with longing to sweep away the whole fabric of society. They think of the inexorable destiny of all; how

> Some gust of jungle wind,
> A stumble on the path, a taint in the tank,
> A snake's nip, half a span of angry steel,
> A chill, a fishbone, or a falling tile,
> And life was over and the man is dead!

and then would fain destroy the good and evil alike, in the myriad convolutions of civilized life, by way of wiping away all tears from the eyes of those who dwell on earth.

It is important to distinguish between the ultimate purposes and the preliminary measures of the leaders of the Social-Democratic Party. Thousands of strong-hearted, weak-headed men join eagerly in measures for the insertion of the thin end of the Socialistic wedge, who would repudiate with horror complicity in the introduction of the thick end.

The thin end of the wedge is summarised by the late Professor Fawcett as follows:—

"After having carefully examined the proposals of the leading German Socialists, and after having read the proceedings of the various Socialistic Congresses which have been held in recent years, I think it will be admitted that the following is a full and fair statement of the programme of modern Socialism:—

"1. That there should be no private property, and that no one should be permitted to acquire property by inheritance. That all should be compelled to labour, no one having a right to live without labour.

"2. The nationalization of the land, and of the other instruments of production; or, in other words, the State should own all the land, capital, and machinery, in fact, everything which constitutes the industrial plant, of a country—in order that every industry may be carried on by the State.

"These proposals to prohibit inheritance,

to abolish private property, and to make the State the owner of all the capital and the administrator of the entire industry of the country, are put forward as representing Socialism in its ultimate and highest development. The Socialists themselves admit that as there is no immediate prospect of obtaining their objects in a complete form, it will be desirable to put forward proposals which involve a less fundamental change, and the following may consequently be regarded as the objects to be first striven for. These objects are regarded as not only desirable in themselves, but are looked upon as facilitating the complete realization of the Socialistic idea :—

"The establishment of co-operative agricultural and manufacturing associations supported by the State.

"Universal, compulsory, and free education.

"3. A progressive income-tax and the abolition of indirect taxation.

"4. The limitation by the State of the length of the day's work.

"5. The sanitary inspection of mines, factories, and workmen's dwellings.

"6. The State should find work for the unemployed by constructing public works, the necessary funds being supplied by an unlimited issue of paper money."

The ultimate purposes of Socialistic policy are :—

1. Abolition of inheritance.
2. Abolition of private property.
3. Abolition of the wages system.
4. Abolition of the competitive system.
5. Government aid to co-operative associations.
6. The institution of paper currency.
7. Abolition of marriage and the family.
8. Abolition of religion.

As, however, any statement of the immediate or ulterior aims of social democracy is not unlikely to be repudiated by some section or other of the party, I have asked Mr. Henry Hyde Champion to state briefly his views on the Socialistic panacea of which he is so courageous and, it must be added, so unselfish an advocate.

"I am asked to briefly state, as one of the Social Democrats in England, my views on these problems. I will not waste words in describing the horrors of our existing society. Where I shall differ from the readers of this book is in ascribing our social ills almost entirely to economical causes over which man has control, and to the consequent material degradation in which the workers have to live. This engenders the disease, folly, and vice which, surely enough, react on the environment and increase the almost hopeless misery. But the first point of the infernal circle is the poverty to which five-sixths of the population are condemned. In other words, uncertainty of employment and low wages for long hours when in work are the main causes of the evils we all profess to deplore. Let any doubting reader think for a moment whether a thousand infants taken from the slums of a great town, and brought up in wholesome physical surroundings, would show, notwithstanding inherited tendencies, such stunted frames, dwarfed intelligences, and warped sympathies as a thousand others who had been left in the slums to be suckled on gin, poisoned by foul air, corrupted by filth and bad food, and crippled by premature toil. No one who clears his mind of illusions can deny that physical health is the basis of moral and mental health, and that all talk of improvement for the masses is the cruellest hypocrisy until their material conditions are altered.

"Why, then, are the workers poor? Social Democracy says, because they have to provide the rent, profits, and interest on which the idlers live; because the modern capitalist form of production forces them to maintain large numbers of useless middlemen; and, because labour-saving machinery, improvements in industry, and gluts due to mad competition throw thousands out of work. For instance, why are the railway and tramway servants wretchedly paid for inhuman hours of work? Simply because those concerns are run in the interest of shareholders whose object is to get dividends by exacting the maximum of work for the minimum of pay. Why are the 800,000 agricultural workers, whose labour, with the aid of sun and rain, creates £240,000,000 of produce annually, constantly "suffering from diseases due to insufficient nourishment?" Because they only get what is left of their produce after satisfying the claims of idlers, speculators, and middlemen. Why are men by the hundred thousand now out of work? Because every improvement in manufacture is used by the capitalist to save wages and because the modern captains of industry in their blind race for wealth overstock the markets. The workers of England can produce more wealth than would provide them with all the means for happy and healthy existence, but they cannot meet the exorbitant demands of the useless classes and have enough left to keep themselves with a sound mind in a sound body.

"The awful condition of the people is recognised by many well-meaning persons, who hope that the classes who profit by long hours, low wages, and the presence of 'the reserve army of labour,' may be persuaded to use the power their property gives them in accordance with the dictates of humanity and the spirit of the Christian religion. They say, in effect, 'Then must the Jew be merciful.' Our modern Shylock answers, 'On what compulsion must I? Tell me that,' and pauses for a reply. Social Democrats (alone, as I think) are ready with an effective one. The only possible conclusion after an examination of the history of class antagonisms in the past is that the workers must compel the idlers to earn their own living by depriving them of the power of preying on others which the possession of land and capital now secures to them. Industry must be organized, not for the profit of the few on a competitive basis, but for the benefit of all by co-operation. This transformation of society—the abolition of classes, the expropriation of the property holders, and the reorganization of industry—is the social revolution we are striving to hasten. 'But the possessing classes will fight rather than surrender their privilege of profiting by the misery and overwork of others'? If so, the workers, thousands of whom are annually killed or mutilated by preventible accidents, who live on the average only half as long as the middle and upper classes, and who compose the army and police, cannot hesitate to choose the risk of sudden death rather than the certainty of life-long misery, when the truth about their position is clear to them and success seems probable. In these-nation, cities how could a determined rising of the victims be suppressed? Does not God fight on the side of the big battalions? It is possible, however, and certainly devoutly to be wished, that the defenders of vested rights will have the wit to calculate the odds, and surrender—as the Irish landlords have done, with bad grace possibly, but without resort to the last argument of force.

"I think I am expressing the opinion of the vast majority of Socialists when I say that there are many practical steps—in the direction of democratising the administration of the country, in extending the control of the community over industry, in limiting the excesses of competition, and in preparing for the reorganization of society on a collectivist system—which we should rejoice to see, while still relentlessly pressing for the complete change: such are adult suffrage, payment of members and of election expenses, the second ballot, shorter parliaments, the nationalization of railways and mines, the municipalization of gas and waterworks and of working-class dwellings, the limitation of the hours of labour, a graduated income tax, free education and the feeding of children in board schools, and the application of our principles to the relief of the unemployed—these things could be done at once, and if carried out in time without the suppression of freedom of the press and platform, might pave the way to a peaceful reconstruction of society.

"Rapidly as the movement is growing in England, we are yet far behind other countries where these views are very popular. This is important, as ultimately Socialism must be international to succeed. Those who are interested in this necessarily curt statement can easily obtain fuller information as to the objects of the English Socialists from the authorised publications of the Social-Democratic Federation."

"The Times," which (according to "Justice") is the organ of the "brothel-frequenting" classes, has presented from time to time with great ability the case for *laissez-faire,* maintaining that all things are for the best in this best of all possible worlds. While the Social Democrats summon the governing classes to face the inevitable downfall of a decaying civilization by a peaceful surrender of all that makes life worth living, "The Times" attracts attention to the improvement in the Nordenfeldt gun, and publishes the recommendations of an expert on the best method of street fighting. The condemnation of skilled mechanics in times of trouble to the disintegration of granite blocks, at a wage of tenpence per diem, creates a sense of the general unfitness of things, which finds expression in an expansive demand for forced community of goods. On the other hand, the fracture of a few club windows impels the owner of property to cry for "resolute government," that he may continue to address to his soul an injunction to take its ease in peace and comfort. There is, I believe, a middle path, and it is on this that I join issue with Mr. Champion and the sanguinary faddists with whom he acts, when they attribute the social horrors we all recognize almost entirely to economical causes. Moral wrong seems to me to lie at the root of the evil, and of this the Social Democrats take no account. The reduction of English Christianity to a caricature of the Sermon on the Mount lends to Mr. Champion and his colleagues a weapon of infinite strength. Christianity says, "Mine is thine." Mr. Champion says, "Thine is mine." Here is the whole difference. Christianity does not fulfil her profession. Mr. Champion is ready to fulfil his. It may be that the ideal is too high; that the rich will always be too sorrowful—without a physical struggle—to part with the portion of goods needed to stay the coming war of classes. Then, and in that case, wild work is ahead, and the struggle can end but in one way.

The case of Robinson Crusoe and his island has often been, and may again be, adduced as an example of the fundamental rights of property. With a nail and a stone he fashions, with infinite toil, a canoe, by which he can visit reefs and islets for crabs and turtle eggs, the wherewithal to mend his fare. Friday, naked and hungry, makes Crusoe's acquaintance, and, admiring the boat and the goatskin clothing, issues the following platform or programme, which is that of the Social Democratic Federation, adapted to the circumstances of Juan Fernandez.

The platform pronounces—

(1). "The establishment of a free condition

of society on Juan Fernandez, based on the principle of political equality, with equal social rights for both."

(2). "The land, with all caves, gardens, bark dwellings, goats, fowls, and other forms of property, to be declared and treated as collective or common property."

(3). "The State appropriation of canoes, and other means of transit, with or without compensation."

Friday presents this programme to Crusoe, and, in justification of his action, quotes the phrase of Lassalle—" To every man according to his needs." Crusoe's reply would depend on his mood. Assuming the discussion to proceed on philosophic lines, he would quote Locke in defence of the property created by the expenditure of labour on raw material. To this Friday might rejoin with Provdhon's well-known dictum, " Property is robbery." Crusoe, not absolutely convinced by Friday's reasoning, may not have the wit, as Mr. Champion says, " to calculate the odds and surrender—as the Irish landlords have done *

* By the way, the Irish landlords have done nothing of the sort.

—with bad grace, possibly, but without resort to the last argument of force." On the contrary, Crusoe will fight, and Crusoe will be right, and the debate will assume the form of a personal encounter. If Crusoe has his cutlass handy, and uses it promptly, Friday will be lucky if he escapes with his life, and anyhow will be convinced by Crusoe that he has cause to regret his fidelity to the principles of the Social-Democratic Federation.

Substitute for Crusoe the eighteen million holders of property in the United Kingdom, and see how much pith and substance there is in Mr. Champion's contention.

Since the anomalous is often that which works best in practice, it is possible to admit all the horrors of the present system without assenting to projects for its total destruction. Of the two evils—(1) Mr. Champion's nihilistic suppression of all moral sanctions, and (2) the juxtaposition of luxury and want as it now exists—the latter seems to be immeasurably the less. But because it is the lesser, is no reason for leaving it alone. Earnest, determined, and continuous efforts by the State on the wholesome lines of the

Ten Commandments, and by all individuals on the softer and sweeter lines of the Mount; to suppress and sterilize the evil-doer by the one, and to visit affliction and redress wrong by the other, if a harder task, is a nobler, and yet more feasible ideal than the pitiless gospel of plunder and insurrection preached by Mr. Champion and his colleagues.

The awful selfishness and bovine content of the comfortable classes—especially of the middle-class—are destined to some such shock as that at which Mr. Champion hints, unless they awake out of sleep. Political economy has been employed too much as though it were an end in itself. Mr. Bright, the Manchester school, and the unrestricted rights of property, have had too long an innings. The premium of insurance paid by property to cover the risk of social earthquake is too low. It must be raised—and that forthwith. The right inherent in every workman to spend, save, and devise the product of his labour, is subject to two moral considerations—one of which is that the process shall not be directly or indirectly the necessary cause of misery to others; and the other, that the duties of property are as inherent as its rights. Sweating toilers, house farmers, and corrupt vestrymen infringe these moral laws. The consequences of their evil-doing, and of the ignorant apathy of the public in abetting them, are visited on the nation by the scandal and the shame that have generated the poisonous propaganda of Social Democracy.

Equality of opportunity does not, in this dispensation, include equality of personality. Under free Governments and by the inexorable decree of the Supreme power, inequality in personality involves inequality in social condition, wealth, knowledge, and power, and such inequalities must therefore exist and continue to exist under all systems of society. Were the Social Democracy to be established to-morrow morning as a Joint-Stock Company wherein everyone is a director, by noontide inequalities in position caused by inequalities in personality would have reappeared. On a level plain every ants' nest is a mountain; every thistle a forest tree. Dynamite the thistles and the ants' nests, and they disappear, only to be succeeded by new generations of ants and thistles.

Competition is inherent in human nature. Pushed too far it leads to wicked cheapness, and costs men's lives and girls' honour. To abolish competition, as the Socialists propose, is to create a new spirit in the hearts of men. This they cannot do, as the constant bickerings in, and secessions from, the Socialist party appear effectively to demonstrate. The desire of Social Democrats to abolish the competitive system, because the consequences of unrestricted competition are deadly to some and hurtful to many, can be compared only with a desire to abolish the use of fire because in many instances lives are lost, limbs maimed, and property destroyed by the cruel license of uncontrolled flames. Competition, like fire, is an excellent servant: when subordinated to the higher laws lying beyond the purview of political economy. Grates, stoves, chimneys, fire bars, bellows, tongs, and water, are needed for the due subjugation of the competitive principle. Tramway men and the white slaves of the tailoring trade in the East End are scorched by the fire of the struggle for existence, and for the infliction of those injuries Society is directly responsible.

The Factory Acts of 1833, 1834, 1844, 1867, 1870, 1878, 1883, are the recognition by Society of common responsibility for the evils of unrestricted competition. It cannot be alleged that there is an essential difference —a difference in principle—between the serfs of sweating tailors or Metropolitan Tramway Companies in 1886, and the Lancashire operatives of 1833. The difference, if any, is one of degree, not of kind. It cannot be difficult, if this be so, to arrive at a principle determining the proper limits for the interference of the State, and defining the circumstances when the interference of the State is injurious alike to the interests of industry and of capital, and to the wholesomeness and independence of national life.

That principle may be briefly stated thus:— *No person or persons are vested with inherent rights to profit arising from the misery and degradation of others.*

Fragmentary acceptances of this principle are scattered up and down the Statute Book. In 48 and 49 Vict., ch. 72, section 12, we have these words :—

"In any contract made after the passing of this Act

for letting for habitation by persons of the working classes a house or part of a house, there shall be implied a condition that the house is at the commencement of the holding in all respects reasonably fit for human habitation."

The missing link in the application of this admitted principle is the pecuniary inability of the poor to set in motion on their own behalf the machinery of the law, and the corruption and apathy of the local authorities who are to the poor *in loco parentis*. Thousands of house-owners in Great Britain are now liable to an action at common law for the insanitary condition of premises let or sublet to working-class tenants since the 14th of August, 1885; and it is probable that they would be cast in heavy damages for neglect of the condition implied in Section 12 of the Housing of the Working Classes Act, 1885. Restricted competition in regard to the disposal of insanitary and dilapidated house property is a palpable admission by the the State that no house-owner has the right to make profits from the letting of houses, the occupation of which is a necessary cause of injury to the occupants.

Unventilated mines, unpointed railways,

ships unseaworthy and half-found, are instances where the intervention of the community in its own protection is already admitted. Once concede that the permanent injury to health and stamina of that class, known to the Social Democrats as " the workers," is an injury to the community as a whole, and the title for interference is complete. The acceptance of the principle I have ventured to formulate would involve a considerable increase to the inspectorial staff, the abolition of the present form of Local government, and a modification of the Employers' Liability Act in the direction of compulsory instead of optional provisions. It will, no doubt, be said that profits will be reduced. This, no doubt, is possibly true; and it is high time that profits should be surrendered when they are obtained only at the cost of national degradation. It is equally probable, however, even on sordid grounds, that the general improvement in the conditions of life of the workers would be profitable to workmen and to capitalists alike.

A surrender of a portion of the profits now legally made must be faced and endured.

The premium of insurance paid by the comfortable classes is not high enough to purchase immunity from spoliation. The strain on the intellect of the poor, when the contrast of poisonous attics and sixteen hours' work with no work and great comfort, is too great for quiet acceptance.

The considerations leading many of the working classes to throw in their lot with the Social Democrats are stated in the following paper, which is being circulated throughout the length and breadth of the kingdom.

Are You a Social Democrat?

If not, you ought to be, for the following reasons:—

Because in this wealthiest country the world has ever seen, vice and misery, ignorance and crime, drunkenness and prostitution, disease and degradation are for the most part the results of want and the fear of want.

Because the average death-rate in the district of St. George's, Hanover Square, and other rich parts of London, is 11 per 1,000, while in poor, overcrowded districts the average death-rate is from 35 to 66 per 1,000.

Because in Manchester and other industrial centres the working classes, on the average, live only half as long as the idle classes.

Because thousands of men in the United Kingdom are killed every year in mines, on railways, and in manufactories by "accidents" which could be prevented if money was spent on improved methods of working.

Because the useful classes in England are forced to work from 60 to 120 hours a week for a bare living, while black slaves were usually only employed 45 hours a week by their masters and were well fed.

Because official Government reports prove that the 800,000 agricultural labourers, who produce more than £240,000,000 worth of food in a year even in these bad times, rarely escape from "diseases due to insufficient nourishment."

Because the Royal Commission on the Housing of the Working Classes found that the children of the poor are brought up under conditions that make health, decency, and morality impossible for them.

Because we have the evidence of John Bright that in Glasgow 70 per cent. of the families have two rooms or less to live, eat, drink, and sleep in.

Because women who work are habitually paid wages on which they cannot live, and there are at least 100,000 prostitutes on the streets of London alone.

Because in every great industry the amount produced per head of those employed has greatly increased, though the number of men in work at these trades has in many cases diminished.

Because it is admitted that children in Board Schools are too badly fed to be well taught without breaking down; and that in one of the poorer districts of London last winter one child out of every three came to school without having had any breakfast.

Because everything that the worker gets to eat, drink, and

wear is made unwholesome by the adulteration for profit, which John Bright says is " a legitimate form of competition."

Because Professor Huxley says that the chief diseases in our great cities are due to slow starvation; and that he would sooner be a savage in the backwoods than an English labourer.

Because Mr. Gladstone says that human life is still for the many a mere struggle for existence.

The statements in this paper are substantially true, and it is pitiful that a poison should be prescribed as a remedy by those who are slowly and surely winning the confidence of the masses: and that the poison should be accepted with avidity, because the natural leaders of the people are silently engaged in other things. Were the middle-classes, with their comfort-worship and their clinging attachment to respectability, to wake out of sleep and to grasp the fact that the next revolution will be directed against them—against the *bourgeoisie*, and not against the aristocracy—all might yet go well. The Local Government of London is the embodiment of the *bourgeois* spirit. What wonder then that Socialists seek the salvation of some in the destruction of all;

would fain visit on the nation the sins of the classes; would atone for selfish indifference by the letting loose of passion; and would seek the reconstruction of society by the destruction of civilization. The handwriting is on the wall. Day by day the characters become more legible. As the ocean murmurs ceaselessly is the murmuring of the people. They are, as Kropotkine says, "a multitude whom no man can number; they are the ocean that can embrace and swallow up all else." Discontent, the daughter of education, breeds resolve; resolve, revolution. Remove from the revolutionist just reason for uprooting the foundations of society, and moral considerations will support the physical measures undertaken in defending property and the old order of society.

Science has immensely strengthened the arm of the individual when raised against society. Explosives, easily manufactured, manipulated by one determined man may at any time change the history of Europe. Fear is no reason for hastening the action of justice. Still, there is every advantage in depriving the dynamitards of the Social-

Democratic party of the semblance of injustice. It must be confessed that much of the responsibility for the blind fury bred of continual woe is to be laid on the shoulders of society. Neglect and hypocrisy conspire to assist the teachings of the communistic *propaganda*. Repair the neglect and sweep away the hypocrisy with resolution and an honest heart, and the Council of the Social Democratic Federation will warble to the unemployed without causing them to twirl in the dance of death.

Again and again the leaders of Socialism have announced their intention of confiscating, in whole or in part, property in land and in all the means of production. Among all their schemes of forced loans, graduated taxes, irredeemable currency, confiscation, and collectivism, there is never found a solitary appeal to the higher sense of the working classes. That much of the misery which appals every thoughtful man arises from idleness as well as from overwork; from too short hours as well as from too prolonged a period of labour; from gluttony and guzzling, as well as from ascetic abstinence;

from reckless unthrift, indulgence, profligacy, and dissipation—does not enter into the Socialistic propaganda. According to them, if a man of the working classes is a voluptuous prodigal within the limits of his capacity and means of enjoyment, he has become so in consequence of the sins of other people. I contend that the idle poor are as distinctly the enemies of the virtuous poor as the idle rich. This, however, is not the Socialist view. With them the remedy for all poverty, arising from whatever cause, is the confiscation of other people's goods.

What is to be done with criminals under the new Co-operative Commonwealth is thus good-humouredly pointed out by Gronlund: "We may now add that not only crimes against property, but all forms of crime will probably be practically unknown."

While human nature is what it is the punishment of idleness ought to consist in allowing free play to the consequences of idleness. A great impulse to the sterilization of the unfit would be given if the idle man were allowed to die unpitied in the street. The crapulous tenderness extended by the nineteenth century to suffering arising from any and from every cause, is the most fertile mother of hereditary pauperism, and all that hereditary pauperism implies. The old Book says, "If a man will not work neither shall he eat." The new edition of the Book, sub-edited to date, absorbs within the scope of its sickly sympathy the misery of the man who will not work. None are better acquainted with the truth of this charge than the industrious poor themselves. We need a wholesome return to that benevolence which was good enough for the prophets and seers of former days. It excluded from the scope of action the interests of the idle man. But the field remaining afforded, and affords, ample play for the finest feelings, for the most devoted energies, for the exercise of the highest capacity, and the display of the most exalted sacrifice. The sinews of our humanity have slackened since it became easier to relieve the idle when they are in trouble, than to seek and to save those who are too proud to ask for alms. As a general rule, the man who can ask charity of strangers is not worthy to receive it. Exceptions naturally occur; but these exceptions are not to be counted as forming a rule. The unfathomable tenderness and wisdom of the Bible never includes in its code of duty the care of the criminally idle.

State-help may be poured into the Socialistic sack until the State is bankrupt, but without self-help and the stimulus of need the pouring out of State aid is done to waste. Self-help gives industrial partnerships, trades'-unions, co-operative and building societies. The demagogues who undermine the self-help which produces these results cannot be counted friendly to the poor man when he offers him as an alternative the million bayonets that will infallibly be raised in defence of family life and the rights of property. Legislation that impairs the spirit of self-help is hostile to social progress. Legislation that restricts the energies of competition so as to allow free play to all competitors develops wholesomely the spirit of self-help.

Whatsoever things are of good report, the greatest deeds in our eight centuries of island-story, the stirring record of many noble lives, and the firm resolve that fills the minds of men of action, are the results of self-help well and rightly exercised. The whinings of the modern school for Jupiter to come down and make all men wise and happy and virtuous by the intervention of the State is a prayer hitherto ungranted, and, if England is to retain what is best in her ancient spirit, will remain ungranted by the new Democracy now and for all time to come.

CHAPTER X.

THE POOR MAN'S BUDGET.

THE typical income of a poor man is that of an average labourer, such as a scaffolder or builder's labourer. A scaffolder possesses a modicum of skill, and earns therefore somewhat higher wages than the hodman or bricklayer's man. Full time is fifty-two hours and a half in a week, which at sixpence an hour amounts to £1 6s. 3d. Assuming that the man is in the prime of life—say thirty years of age—he will probably be married and have a family of three children. Wages are paid at noon on Saturday, and he will probably there and then drink, or treat his mates to an average of, two pots of beer at fourpence a pot; and he will spend on beer and tobacco together not less than five shillings a week on the average of one week with another. Although it is not the custom to give credit for drink at public-houses, it is not unusual to do so at beer-houses, where a request to "stick it up" is seldom refused if the customer be known, and is in work. Some publicans refuse to give credit for drink, as they are unable to sue for tippling debts. They, therefore, evade the statute by lending the drinker the equivalent of his debt in cash, and then, in the event of his being unable or unwilling to pay, they sue him for money lent. The practice of gambling for drink with dominoes is unusual in what are known as "stand-up" houses, or houses where spirits are sold; but dominoes are often kept in beer-houses for the purpose of enabling the landlord's customers to determine by resort to a game of chance the person upon whom the burden of payment should fall. The usual drink is colloquially known as "four-ale," so called because it is fourpence a pot, and this, divided with "four-half," which is a mixture of porter, or black beer, and "four-ale,"

P

obtains the suffrages of most of the drinkers. If this beer be drunk off the premises and is sent for in the customer's jug the price will be reduced to threepence-halfpenny a pot, or sometimes to threepence. In the opinion of some intelligent working men, beershop-keepers are bound to doctor their beer in order to pay rates, rent, and taxes; the beer thus treated is said to be "faked," and on Saturday and Sunday, more than on any other part of the week, the occult treatment of beer is in operation. The sales are larger on these two days than on any other two days in the week, especially in the lower houses, and it is alleged that many publicans, and most barmen, have their especial secrets for the treatment of the beverages received from the brewer. Beershop-keepers devote a regular portion of their time to the management of their cellars, and the analysis of beer sold on Saturday night, or after church time on Sunday, would be interesting. The labourers of the building trade who have often to relinquish work, especially in the spring, in consequence of rain, are attracted to those beershops where they can get credit;

and in the lower class of houses the beershop-keeper is generally a pot-boy or barman who has risen from the ranks, and is not seldom a cunning and selfish member of the community.

Although beer in its various forms is most constantly drunk, other beverages chiefly consumed are gin—as being the cheapest, and therefore more easily sophisticated—and rum and new whisky. A not unusual consumption of beer for an average labourer is half-a-pint at eleven a.m., one pint at one p.m., half-a-pint at three p.m., and a pint and a half after tea, that would come to four shillings and a penny a week, leaving elevenpence for tobacco, and no margin for getting drunk. Complaints are rife that some of the beer is terribly bad, it creates thirst, and even a small quantity involves a morning headache.

The price of gin is from fourpence-halfpenny to fivepence per quartern. Although it is usual for potmen of neighbouring beerhouses to visit bricklayers and labourers on small building jobs, drinking is not allowed on large jobs, which are therefore not so popular among a large class as those of more restricted dimensions. The character of the liquor supplied varies with the character of the public-houses.

Taking, then, four shillings and a penny as the average weekly expenditure on drink by a labourer throughout the year, it appears that he spends in the course of a year £10 12s. 4d. As he pays twopence a pint for his beer it is evident that he loses by retail consumption. Taking the price of a nine-gallon cask of pure beer at ten shillings, if he were able to buy seventeen nine-gallon casks of beer instead of 1,274 pints he would have about £2 2s. 4d. in hand, which would be a valuable addition to the fund available for schooling, clothes, or food, without reducing the consumption of liquor he is accustomed to enjoy.

The tobacco smoked by the labourer is almost exclusively known as shag. Shag tobacco is generally bought over the bar of the public-house, at twopence the half-ounce or a penny the "screw." Assuming that the weight is accurately measured, which is by no means always the case, the price per pound avoirdupois of this shag tobacco would be five shillings and fourpence. A labourer will smoke three ounces a week in the year of fifty-two weeks. This makes 156 ozs., which at fourpence an ounce is £2 12s.; if he were to buy his tobacco a pound at a time instead of in small quantities, apart from the loss by weight, which is often considerable, he would have a further sum of sixteen shillings available for the general purposes of a family, without reducing the quantity of tobacco in which he indulges. Most labourers have a pipe in their mouths whenever possible. As a class they smoke more than mechanics. Investigations I have made as to the proportion of smokers show that no fewer than from ninety to ninety-four per cent. of labourers, whether in or out of work, either smoke or chew.

The rent is a heavy item, and accommodation generally bad. The model dwellings, especially the Peabody Buildings, are not inhabited by labourers, and it is hardly too much to say that at present the accommodation for men of the lower wage-earning class has not been touched by the provision of model dwellings. If our scaffolder is an Irishman he will probably live in one room, for which he pays not less than four shillings a week; and if he pays his rent regularly he is not only profitable to his "middleman" landlord, but is paying to the latter an insurance against the delinquencies of other tenants. Next to the matter of obtaining work the rent question is regarded as the most important by the labouring classes; there is no privation through which they will not pass rather than break up their home, and their efforts to pay their rent are often necessarily attended by a diminution in their supply of food needful for subsistence. Arrears of rent are more feared than any other form of debt, and it is not improbable that the class most benefited by the creation of Mansion House Funds are the tenement landlords of London. There is very little doubt that the hatred and execration with which landlords throughout the country are generally regarded by the uneducated portion of the proletariat is the result of contact with one form of landlord, who is too often a middle-man or sub-lessee without capital, and who is not seldom devoid of those qualities for which many of the great landowners of England and Ireland have obtained the confidence and affection of their country tenants. Subjoined is a letter illustrative of this point :—

"Dear Sir,
"I hope you will pardon me for the liberty I take in writing to you. I had to get —— to write before, as I was not able to, sir. I take the liberty of asking you if you can assist me in my present trouble. I had the misfortune of doing a very little work since Christmas, which caused me to get back in my rent. Second, my misfortune, taken ill has still made it worse for me, making three months at three shillings per week I owe, sir. My landlord is bad; he has got five little houses down where I live. He told me on Monday he could get no rent; he cannot get enough out of them to pay the taxes, so he's going to turn them out and sell the houses; so he has told me that if I do not pay him some this week he will put my things into the street. Sir, if you will assist me this time I will not trouble you again. Sir, I have two loaves and 1s. 6d. in grocery from the parish for me, my wife, and five children

for a week, so you see, sir, we cannot afford to waste much of that; so if you will be so kind as to send me a little money to help me out of my present trouble I shall be thankful."

"From your humble servant,

"———."

There is a curious preference on the part of most labourers for living in a room in a small house as compared with a large barrack-like building. It is for this reason that, while the competition for unlet rooms in small tenement houses is invariably keen, few, if any, of the model dwellings situated in the midst of a dense population are fully let; the restrictions as to cleanliness, the disposal of rubbish, the washing and drying of clothes, and the regulations as to sanitary arrangements are repugnant to the free-born Englishman or Irishman, or, rather to the ladies of his family; and they will prefer to pay more for a small room where they are let alone, than for apartments in a poor man's palace, where they are inspected and harassed by injunctions to a cleanly and an orderly life. There is always a charm in Alsatia; and those of the tenement landlords of London who make their pound of flesh the chief object in life are thoroughly aware of this fact, trade on it, and reap their reward. Of the £10 8s. paid as rent, therefore, I estimate that at least £1 0s. 9d. is paid over and above the amount necessary to replace capital, a sinking fund for depreciation, and interest of five per cent.; but it is difficult to say how the poor man's budget can be reduced on the expenditure side by this amount until the Legislature takes vigorous measures with regard to the alienation of responsibility to sub-lessees by superior landlords.

Butcher's meat is generally enjoyed on Sunday only, when it is either bought for cash at the cheap butcher's on Saturday night, or at small chandler's shops, which now supply bread, meat, and milk, as well as tea, bacon, sugar, oatmeal, butter, and flour. Minute quantities of food are sold at these chandlers' shops. Milk, for example, can be obtained at one farthing the half-quartern—that is, the eighth of a pint. Fish is eaten on Friday, even by Protestants, but it is not considered nourishing, and there is no great liking for it in any form, unless fried, and this mostly among the lads and young men. In the evenings the fried fish shops are crowded by this latter class, who make a hearty meal on the odoriferous viands prepared in full view.

The dinner taken by our scaffoldman to his work will generally consist of bread and cheese with a rasher of bacon on most days, with perhaps some cold meat on Monday, the remains of Sunday's dinner. If the wife goes out during the week to earn a shilling or two by some cleaning or charing work, he will mend his fare with meat in the course of the week. The appetites of these out-of-door labourers are enormous, unless they are addicted to drink more heavily than the typical case of a man whose budget is being considered.

To maintain the family health, viz., two adults and three children, will cost not less than thirteen shillings a week, of which not less than one shilling is the tribute to defective methods of distribution.

The next item of importance is coals. These are obtained in small quantities;

often as little as 7lbs. avoirdupois being fetched at one time. The price of this coal is one penny for 7lbs., which amounts to £1 6s. 8d. a ton. The coal is generally inferior, some of it dust, and a good deal of slag or stone. About one quarter of a hundredweight will be used daily, and will cost a shilling to fifteenpence per week; he will thus spend about £3 0s. 8d. in fuel in the course of the year, including wood, candles, and matches; the former of these he often obtains as an acknowledged perquisite from the place where he is employed. Thirty-seven per cent. of this expenditure is due to imperfect distribution, as the coal for which he pays at the rate of £1 6s. 8d. per ton would not be worth, if delivered by the ton, more than fifteen or sixteen shillings, and this notwithstanding that our scaffoldman or some member of his family has to fetch his coal from the greengrocer's or chandler's shop.

Clothes form the next item, which, at least in the summer time, is less serious than the provision of boots. Children's clothing is bought in Leather Lane and Somers Town cheaply, by middle-men from factors, and resold on Saturday night or Sunday morning in the open street or at small wardrobe shops at considerable profit. The price, however, of these clothes is but small, and the expenditure one week with another does not exceed fifteenpence a week for the family. With boots, however, the matter is different. Boots are a necessity to the bread-winner, and there is considerable shame felt if the children are obliged to attend school shoeless, or with their foot-coverings in an unusually dilapidated condition. It is not unusual to contract with a shoemaker for a contract supply of boot leather for the family all the year round, including repairs, at a sum not exceeding a shilling or fourteenpence a week.

The budget expenditure for the week now amounts to £1 5s. 8d., leaving sevenpence for newspapers, indulgences, treats, holidays, presents, subscriptions, club, music-hall, pew-rent, postage, books, charity, hospitality, repair of furniture, and other incidentals of family life. It will thus be seen that intermission of work, or the confinement of the house-mother, or illness of the bread-winner will plunge the family in the full blast of the north wind. A resort to the pawnshop is, in such an event, a matter of necessity, and here the loans of the poor man are only effected on payment of interest which would be regarded as usurious in another class of society. A movement has been made lately for the purpose of introducing into England the system of the Mont du Piété, and at all events it can hardly be denied that " The Pawnbrokers" Act of 1872 needs revision.

The direct or indirect taxes paid by the scaffolder to the State are very small, except on spirits, beer, tobacco, and tea. He is more lightly taxed than his Continental brother. But of his income of £68 5s., assuming he is in work all the year round, he pays £7 9s. 1d. in virtue of his inability to purchase many household requisites and his own luxuries at the same rate as is possible to those possessing capital.

From this state of things it is evident that retail quantities of stores at wholesale prices is the principal method by which society can help the poor working man. Co-operation in the ordinary sense of the term involves proprietary interest and permanent residence.

Neither of these conditions is present in the case of the scaffolder. No spare cash is available for investment, and he is nomadic in his habits by the exigencies of his work. Twenty per cent. of the London electorate changed their residences between November, 1885, and July, 1886; the majority of these changes being the poorer class of the voters.

It is therefore essential, if the blessings of co-operation (which have proved so signally useful to the residential artizans and millhands of the Midland counties) are to be extended to the poor urban population, that the organization and administration must be undertaken and the funds provided by others. Some, at all events, of the poor shop-keepers who would be disestablished by the change could be engaged as salesmen. For ten thousand pounds the retail meat trade of the East End could be revolutionized in favour of the indigent customer. Under any circumstances it would be well, were funds available for such a purpose, to proceed strictly on commercial lines, and to divorce the measures taken from the taint of ineffective philanthropy.

CHAPTER XI.

THE UNEMPLOYED.

THE one feature of the permanent distress ruling amongst the working classes, to which public notice is most forcibly drawn, is the existence of a large and destitute class, outside the poor-houses, without employment or visible means of existence. This plant of evil growth ripens in the winter; not only because the building trades cease, and the summer occupations of casual labourers come to a standstill, but because the physical contrast presented between the lives of capitalists and of labourers, at this season of the year, is too vivid to be wholly ignored. The customary method of expressing a sense of sympathy with labour in distress is the performance of a winter masquerade at the Mansion House, by which pauperization of the people is rubbed into their lives a little more deeply, and the flames of hatred between the Haves and the Not-haves fanned a little higher. Opinion is divided as to the real effect of these hurriedly obtained funds. Optimists hold that, by collecting in panic and distributing in haste, society has nobly done its duty to the poor. Pessimists contend that the wrong people manage to obtain the bulk of the money, and that so far as the administration of such a fund has any effect at all, the effect is wholly and indisputably evil. It is probable that the truth lies midway between the optimist and the pessimist point of view—that neither real good nor immediate harm accrues from the distribution of a few shillings to families in a chronic state of misery and degradation. It is difficult to understand how either immediate good or immediate harm can result from the distribution of a few pence or shillings to people who, after consuming the charity, are neither better nor worse for having enjoyed it. A moderate estimate places the number of souls in London who are at hand-grips with necessity at half a million. Seventy thousand pounds divided among this multitude amounts to two shillings and sevenpence each. It is probable that the only permanent effect of a Mansion House fund is to burden the next generation with a few hundreds of the unfit, who, but for the existence of the fund, would either never have entered the world, or would have gone out of it under the irresistible operation of natural law. The fecundity of starving people is notorious, and has again and again been exemplified in famine districts in India. A policy based on relief from funds collected in a hurry, and administered by machinery raised in a night, can be but a temporary policy. The evil grows by what it feeds on. We may therefore look forward with some certainty to the final discredit and breakdown of the system of meeting the unemployed problem by cheque charity. The one justification for a Mansion House emergency fund is the patient and contemporaneous construction of machinery for permanently dealing with the question.

The saddest side of the unemployed problem is the existence of a large and growing class of persons who refuse to be driven by any privation to seek assistance from the Poor Law. The independence and resolve evinced by such a spirit deserve the support of the community. Governments bent on maintaining a sense of manly independence in the people would, in the long days of summer, prepare for the inevitable strain of winter troubles. Any relaxation of the rule which requires as a condition of relief to able-bodied male persons the entry to the workhouse, or the performance of an adequate task of work as a labour test, would be disastrous. Such relaxation would tend to restore the vicious state of things before the reform of the Poor Laws, when the independence of the labouring classes had practically ceased to exist, and the poor-rates were increased so as to become an insupportable burden.

Distress in London is not the distress of a great city—it is the distress of a great Empire. If a Yorkshire yokel is dismissed from employment because machinery performs work formerly effected by men, he is as likely to come to London as to Leeds. Distressed British seamen from all parts of the world make for the Port of London. If I am right in contending that the imperial character of metropolitan distress destroys any just comparison between it and the distress of provincial towns, the conclusion is inevitable that exceptional—because imperial distress—can be met only by exceptional—that is, by imperial measures.

There are two considerations which lend support to the view now advanced, upon which some detailed examination will not be out of place.

The Government of the City of London glories in a great historic position, and in the possession of privileges more extended than those of any town in the Empire. It shares the administration of the province of houses from which it derives its name, with the Metropolitan Board of Works, Vestry Boards, District Boards, the Home Office, the Local Government Board, and the Social-Democratic Federation. The only municipality in London is the Corporation of the City, and although it enjoys a complete power of internal reform, it retains customs inconsistent with the principles of the Municipal Corporations Act. As a matter of fact, and possibly in consequence of clinging to the forms of other days, the Corporation of London is out of touch with the main body of the citizens; and its place, as the leader and mouthpiece of the capital of the Empire, is not filled either by the Metropolitan Board of Works or any of the vestries or boards who, by a fiction of the law, are credited with exercising the functions of the local authorities. The net result of the confusion and rivalry existing between the various bodies charged with the administration of the affairs of London, is the administrative impotence of the Capital in such matters as providing for the unemployed, but which is done with complete success in Birmingham, Glasgow, and other great cities in the United Kingdom.

Since there is no municipality to whom the unemployed can address themselves, it follows that, pending the creation of a London Government, the Queen's Minister is, whether he likes it or not, *in loco parentis* to the unmanageable masses of unemployed gathered on the poor man's side of the Thames.

The other argument for invoking temporarily the action of the Government under the special and exceptional circumstances of the case, is the fact that the provision of a Mansion House fund, which averts civil war for the time being, not only falls on a few generous, patriotic, and public-spirited citizens whose names are found in every good work, but it relieves the Vestries and the Boards of Guardians from duties thrown on them by the law, and which they are only too anxious and willing to evade. The guardians of the poor, in guarding the rates, become the guardians of the rich rather than of the poor.

Before entering into the consideration of what can be done for the permanent benefit of the unemployed, it will be well to analyse the materials from which the army of unemployed is created. The analysis I am about to give is the result of personal examination into the circumstances of about six thousand men, who, presumably unable to afford fourpence for shelter in a common lodging-house, were found wandering throughout the winter nights foodless and without a place to lay their heads. I do not pretend that this analysis is exhaustive, or that more value should be attached to the opinion of a mere individual than is deserved by an effort to arrive at truth at the cost of many all-night wanderings in the streets of London during the winter season.

Forty per cent. of these night nomads were, in a national sense, hopelessly submerged. They were often affected with disease, infected with lice, and bore the marks of Cain upon their countenance. They are the pariahs of civilization. Irregular meals, uncleanly habits, and the loathly environment in which they live, render them physically incapable of doing an honest day's work. Petty crimes are perpetrated by people of this class as one means of existence, and they are partly maintained by the system of bat-eyed benevolence which gratifies its own selfish emotions at the cost of generations to come. The casual wards always contain specimens of this class. They are the unfittest of the unfit, and are to be dealt with permanently only by sterilization. For this purpose they must be regarded as the enemies of society, and, as in the case of repeatedly convicted criminals, should be segregated for life, or until such time as the danger to posterity from the perpetuation of their species had passed away.

The next 40 per cent. have not fallen to so low a level. Emaciated with want, they retain some moral sense of the dignity of manhood. They are capable of performing two or three hours' work of descriptions not demanding the exercise of skill. But their labour does not possess such competitive value as would enable them to assume a serious part in the work of the world. Intimate relations seem to exist between the physical and moral states of this class of the unemployed. Fed and clothed into fitness and decency, they quickly become as other men are, and resume the cheery demeanour and alertness characteristic of the Londoner when relieved from the pressure of immediate want. There is not much that can be done by public means for the benefit of the majority of the class now under review. The function of the State is not primarily to save the lives of the unfit—from whatsoever cause unfitness may arise. They are proper subjects for the personal friendship of those with whom fortune has been more kindly. A cheque from an unknown hand, absorbed in the maalström of a central fund, dispensed under ironclad rules by scientific hands, excites neither gratitude nor surprise. Let every man and woman who can do so seek out and save, by personal contact and patient sympathy, some poor soul blighted by hereditary taint, or maimed by the cold steel of the Manchester school cheapness-worship. Sharing will be found far more effectual than doling, and more seemly as between friends. There is a house in the West End of London, full of art and beauty, where the harvest of the eye is full and rich. From time to time this house is opened to the poor men and poor women, whose usual lot is to be wedged in the hopeless dulness of the East End. Not served below stairs with condescending patronage, but welcomed as honoured guests in beautitul reception-rooms, among the palms and the orchids, the *tazze,* and the paintings, many a poor man has first dimly learned the lesson that, after all, the true brotherhood is not inconsistent with orders and rank in society; and that differences in birth, culture, and intelligence, are no bars to a common faith in the Teacher of the Mount, and to the practice of His teachings.

The larger portion of the remaining 20 per cent. consists of soldiers. Large numbers of men who have served the Queen in recent campaigns are compelled on wet and snowy nights to tramp the streets because they have nowhere to get a crust or a shelter. Trades are not learned in the army so as to enable ex-soldiers to compete with skilled and energetic men engaged for the whole of their lifetime in the practice of one employment. Trades acquired in the services do not, except in special cases, enable the learners to obtain a subsequent livelihood. Many men leaving the army are practically homeless, and as the scanty store of money taken with them melts away, they gravitate to the banks of the Thames, and become rivals for work, which only one in three can succeed in obtaining.

It would be impertinent to express an opinion as to the military effect of the short-service system. The effect, however, on the condition of the lives of the poor has been disastrous, from all points of view. A man who is fit to serve the Queen must be physically and morally superior to the vast proportion of the urban population into which he sinks when discharged from his regiment. His discharge is attended, in the majority of instances, by relapse into hopeless poverty. The number of soldiers among the unemployed is appalling. They crowd the casual wards, and are found in every employment where skill is not required. The efforts of these poor fellows to obtain work are as gallant as their active service; but they are weighted with the burden of a career, which, however honourable on the lips of festive speakers after dinner, disables them in their search for employment. If a man is borne on the roll of the first or second class of the Army Reserve, his chance of employment is lessened; for, since every petty *émeute* abroad has involved calling up the second line of defence—as much as though we were menaced with grave national danger —employers naturally refrain from engaging men who at any moment are liable to be withdrawn from positions of more or less trust and importance. Sometimes the anguish of mind following the hopeless search for work induces men who have faithfully served Queen and country, and who have been turned on to the world with a good character and with enough to retard quick starvation, to end their troubles by self-destruction. In July, 1886, the suicide of an ex-soldier was reported in a brief newspaper paragraph between a description of the *escapade* of a fashionable actress and a list of the winning mounts of a fashionable jockey. In the pocket of the corpse was a paper, and written on it were these words:—" Died of a broken heart; unable to get work."

So long as England is able to buy for seventy thousand pounds a picture, considered by some critics not of the highest class, or to defend one Irish landlord at a cost to the country of three thousand pounds a year, the needless death of one man who has served his country, and the general condition of the whole class of ex-soldiers, is a stain on the character of the country. I do not believe it is the will of the English people that men who have served the Queen, especially those who have faced danger of foreign foe in battle, or of a pestilential climate, should be cast out like drafted hounds. If any man be entitled to employment by the State, surely it is he who has served the State, in danger to himself, both well and faithfully. The minor posts in the civil service should be reserved for competent men of good character discharged from the army, and should no longer be dealt with by the patronage of ministers, or wholly in conformity with the teachings of the Manchester school.

Another component portion of the twenty per cent. of the unemployed now being considered is the class of men who have been artizans earning their living by skill in the use of tools. Too large a family, illness, or depression of trade, and the compulsory sale of tools, have forced them to relinquish the exercise of skill, and sink into the ranks of mere labourers. The sufferings of these men are acute: and their pluck and patience is most pathetic. Unaccustomed, as agricultural labourers are accustomed, to hard and grinding toil, they quickly become submerged, never to regain their former position. Often they are men whose minds are equipped with some measure of education, and they are proudly resolute not to taint their mouths with workhouse bread. Alms are sometimes offered to this class, and the hand that offers it is cursed, while the proffered gift is refused with scorn. These are the men who form the most effective material in the manufacture of the Social-Democratic party. Failure only partly attributable to the community is by them placed wholly on the shoulders of Society—and nothing short of industrial revolution is held by them to be a satisfactory or adequate solution of the problems of their bitter lives.

Then come the agricultural labourers from all parts of the kingdom, who in entering London exchange a hard lot for one that is hopeless. The whisper of a Mansion House fund blackens the North Road with swarms of these poor fellows, who, aimlessly and unprevented, swell the ranks of the competitive army of the soldiers of unskilled labour. In three months their rural characteristics have disappeared, and in six they are permanently absorbed into the floating population of the great city.

The only method of dealing with the agricultural classes who flock to the towns, attracted by the magnetism of a great mass, is to divert them from the country to the Colonies. Emigration is practically at a standstill. Colonization, therefore, is the only method of dealing with the surplus rural population, and there is perhaps no method by which the permanent good of all classes of the community is more effectually secured, than by the organization of settlement such as that dealt with in the chapter on Colonization.

This analysis of a few thousands of night nomads shows that besides the soldiers and the agricultural labours, to be dealt with by colonization and State employment respectively, there is a large body of men who have drifted to London as much from thoughtlessness as from design. These people being rooted in the Metropolis, are those upon whom the punishment of a cold winter and general depression tells with the most unerring certainty. The labour test usually imposed by the parish authorities is stone-breaking or oakum-picking. This work is selected as offering but little competition with other labour. But it presses hardly on skilled artizans, and impairs their proficiency in their own trades. Spade labour is less open to objection, but it is not often that Guardians are either able or willing to supply the unemployed with the opportunity of working with the spade or shovel. What is required is work that all able-bodied men can perform; which does not compete with other employments; and which is not likely to interfere with the resumption of regular employment in their own trades by those who are compelled by necessity to seek for aid. As regards the East End parishes, it is not reasonable to expect that ratepayers should bear the burden of providing relief works for men who, as has been shown, flock in from all parts of the Empire. East End rates are normally higher than the rates of other parts of London. Pending the equalization of the rates for the whole of the metropolis, it is not likely that local authorities will willingly embark in schemes for the relief of distress accidentally falling within the area of their own administration. The belated advice of the Local Government Board, from time to time distributed with ineffectual wisdom, is naturally ignored. The Board has no power of constraint.

It is difficult to resist the conclusion that under the special circumstances of the case, *i.e.,* the absence of a Municipality for London, the impotence of the local authorities, and the grave evils attending the helter-skelter administration of charitable funds— the Government must accept a responsibility in London which they do not seek to evade in India. Plans for the employment of Indian labour in districts liable to famine are in readiness throughout the three Presidencies. I fail to see why provisions held to be necessary in the case of our Hindoo and Mahometan fellow-subjects should be superfluous or unwise when dealing with Englishmen and their families. Irish distress is articulate through the voices of Irish Members of Parliament, and measures for the relief of distress in the sister island receive the approval of all parties and of all creeds. What is done for Ireland and for India should not be left undone for London.

If, on reviewing all the circumstances of the case, spade labour be considered most suitable to the needs of a starving population, the defences of London would appear the most appropriate object for the expenditure of funds intended to be applied to the relief of distress. It cannot be pretended that relief works of this nature would be pecuniarily remunerative. It is undesirable that they should be directly remunerative. The erection of forts and earth-works would compete with no other employment ; would not involve the possession of skill ; and would be carried out beyond the confines of the metropolitan area. Payment should be made largely in kind, and, if necessary, the Truck Act should be modified with this object. No Act of Parliament would be needed for the erection of forts on land already in possession of the War Office, and preparations for the camp of labour to be employed can be organized in a few weeks. Ministries have again and again incurred expenditure on wars, and preparations for war, for which they were subsequently obliged to obtain an indemnity from Parliament. There appear to be no fundamental objections to the plan of temporarily providing for the able-bodied unemployed by completing the defences of London. The rates of wages paid, either in money or in kind, should be so arranged as not to attract labourers from other employments, and idlers refusing the honourable work thus provided should be allowed to take the consequences of their idleness. The habit of idleness is so rooted in the nature of a small portion of the population that they will incur privation, resort to malingering, steal—in short, do anything rather than apply themselves to win their bread by the sweat of their brow.

It is probable that the organization of relief works on some such plan as this would reduce the distress of able-bodied men to manageable dimensions. The wives and families of the men employed would no doubt need assistance, which could be rendered by arranging for the payment to the wives of a portion of the wages earned by the men on the same system of deposit notes and remittances as is adopted on behalf of seamen in the navy and mercantile marine. The work would be of so hard and disagreeable a nature that none would resort to it except in extremity. On the other hand the taint of the poor-law and workhouse relief would be abolished, and men employed would preserve their independence in reflecting that the work on which they were engaged was one of national importance and of the highest necessity.

Some military authorities are of opinion that the creation of a system of defence for the metropolis and its approaches is by itself a matter that should no longer be postponed, and that without reference to the state of the labour market the accessibility of London to hostile forces constitutes a grave and national danger. Whether or not this view of the case be correct, it is clear that there is an opportunity of ensuring the safety of London and of its prodigious wealth under circumstances exceptionally favourable to the National Exchequer, and at the same time of reducing the proportions of a calamity with which we are menaced from within.

To recapitulate some of the measures

needed to solve the problem of the unemployed, the following steps may be among those to be adopted with advantage :—

(1). The institution under War Office management of a system of metropolitan defences.

(2). The organization of agricultural settlements in the Colonies for labourers driven from the soil.

(3). The employment of ex-soldiers in the petty offices of the civil service.

(4). The administration of charity, whenever practicable, by the givers themselves or their agents, and under no circumstances resort to centralized funds, care being taken by organization to prevent "over-lapping."

CHAPTER XII.

CHARITIES.

THE annual revenue of the metropolitan charities is greater than the whole of the expenditure in Sweden, on maintaining royalty, the administration of justice and foreign affairs, Army and Navy, internal, educational, and ecclesiastical affairs, and in providing interest on the Swedish debt. It is difficult to say whether in the long run the community would be benefited or prejudiced by the complete and immediate stoppage of all charitable subscriptions to benevolent societies. On the one hand, acute suffering would be caused to individuals, though the death of many of the unfit would be advantageous to succeeding generations. Large bodies of clerks, secretaries, and salaried administrators would be thrown out of employment, but the money employed in paying them would be available for more useful objects. Looking to the large sums expended in London charities, and to the amount of distress ascertained to exist, it is probable that the money actually provided is more than sufficient to meet the necessities of those who are proper subjects for the exercise of private charity.

The defects in the present system of charitable administration are three in number: (1) the competition raging between weak institutions carrying on similar work with separate machinery; (2) the enormous sums wasted in administrative expenses and advertisements; (3) the absence of any palpable relation between charitable work and endowment and their effects on the solution of the social problem, and therefore on the welfare of the community. Take, for example, the sum of £312,000 a year which is expended on institutions for General Relief. No doubt much individual misery is temporarily relieved. The other side of the picture lies in the wholesale destruction of the sense of parental responsibility for the physical and mental welfare of children brought into the world, and the creation of confirmed habits of dependence on charitable doles in a class increasing its numbers with greater rapidity than the independent and self-supporting classes from which the bone and sinew of the nation are recruited.

With regard to the competition between charitable institutions pursuing identical aims, the evil is not so great. The mere waste of money, and the prostitution of a sacred idea, exhibited in the profane avidity with which rival institutions clamour for public help are not matters of national importance. Take, for example, the twenty-six charities for the Blind, costing £55,677 a year. It is impossible not to believe that improved administration, greater economy, and increased usefulness would result from a fusion between the different interests, conducted on lines precisely similar to those followed in the case of Railway or Insurance Companies, where the proprietory is bent on effecting an amalgamation between rival interests.

Or take the £108,470 a year spent on twenty-nine miscellaneous special hospitals. It is difficult for a layman to understand what advantage can accrue to the community—whatever may be the effect on the interests of individual specialists—in the multiplication of the existing hospital system by miscellaneous special hospitals issuing separate appeals to the public for support. It should be explained that besides the seventeen General Hospitals, commanding the support of the charitable, there are eight Consumption Hospitals, five Ophthalmic, three Orthopedic, three Skin, twenty-one for Women and Children, and six Lying-in Hospitals. In addition to these, twenty-nine miscellaneous hospitals, to which objection is taken, are instituted for the most part with special reference to the diseases of particular organs, which can be as efficiently, and certainly more widely and economically, studied and treated in a large General than in a small Special hospital. The medical profession have deserved so well, and have received so little from the community, as compared with the legal and the clerical professions, it is somewhat invidious to venture on suggestions for the reorganization of a portion of the existing medical machinery of the metropolis. The first and almost the special point in which civilization contrasts with barbarism, consists in the tenderness and care bestowed on infirm, unfit, and undesirable lives, tainted with disease or maimed with deformity. Whether on the whole the results of applying medical science to the maintenance and preservation of the unfit, and of improving the sanitary conditions of daily life, are, or are not, on the whole advantageous to the community, need not here be discussed. The compassionate feelings of the wealthier classes lead them to subscribe nearly £600,000 a year for the benefit of ninety-two hospitals in the metropolis. The question is therefore whether a federation could not be established between the administrations of separate mechanisms for identical objects, with the view of dispensing from time to time with certain hospitals where the work can be carried on as efficiently and more economically in larger institutions.

The subject of charities cannot be touched

without reference to those semi-fraudulent institutions conducted primarily as a means of existence for their promoters, and not for the relief of the poor. Under the present system any letter or advertisement in the daily papers, or a circular to the public appealing for funds for charitable purposes, may be inserted or issued without let or hindrance. The law intervenes only in the event of the mal-administration of such funds, attracting sufficient public attention to demand investigation and inquiry under the Criminal Law. So numerous are these appeals, that the time has arrived when no one should be permitted to make a public appeal for charitable funds without being subjected to the ordeal of a Public Audit.

The multiplication of weak institutions seems not unlikely to receive greater impulse during the jubilee year of Her Majesty's reign. It were to be desired that that historic event could be perpetuated by the rearrangement and concentration on scientific principles of the funds obtained, and of the institutions already in existence, rather than by the extraction of more funds from the public pocket, and by the erection of additional institutions for the purpose of doing that which is already being done in other quarters.

The need for charity should diminish from the hour that the Problems of a great City begin to undergo the process of solution. The poor we have always with us. But the continuity of their existence is no ground for making systems of relief the instruments for propagating pauperism, destroying thrift, relieving parents of their duties, and generally subsidising the powers of darkness. Objectively considered, the existence of two or more charitable agencies occupying the same ground at the same time, is as irrational as if numerous water companies were to engage in the supply of water to a single street. Either harmonious concert must exist between rival charities—which notoriously is not the case—or some of the objects of charitable relief will be neglected, and others will be superfluously assisted. The Society for the Organization of Charitable Relief implies by the ambition of its title that it has undertaken the task of welding duplicate undertakings, pruning exuberant energies, and mapping out the areas in which the force of disciplined generosity can usefully expend itself. Grappling with a task of enormous difficulty, it is not surprising that the Society for the Organization of Charitable Relief has neither equalled the intentions nor adhered to the ideal of its founders. Through evil report it has, however, steadily pursued with English tenacity one of the objects with which it was founded, although the public mind is confused by the incongruity of its functions. One would think that an organization created to arrange and marshal disunited energy, would refrain from itself competing as a relief agency with the very societies it proposes to organize. Weighty and experienced minds are associated with the Society for the Organization of Charitable Relief, and to them the public may fairly look for a new departure in the direction indicated by the title of the Society. Mansion House Local Committees have shown that in times of distress religious and political animosities can be laid aside under the pressure of public calamity, and under the influence of a common sympathy. Permanent charitable committees might well be organized by whom not only the administration of charitable relief should be undertaken within the area allotted for their operations, but from whom should proceed a permanent stream of appropriate criticism of the local authorities when neglect or corruption are shown to exist. It has been already shown in the case of the Emigration Societies how puerile and wasteful is the system of numerous disunited and feeble efforts. The circumstances detailed in the case of the Emigration Societies apply to many other forms of charitable endeavour. Preliminary to better administration, must be intelligent contact between the various circles of charitable influence. The English public is compassionate as a woman when its emotions are really stirred. But the essence of the problem of administering the immense revenue annually raised remove the question from emotional to intellectual regions. That which is required, therefore, is the continuous application on the spot of the same class of mind to the charitable problem, as is bestowed on the building and command of our ships;

on the administration of our railway system, the economical and successful conduct of the complex operations of a large and successful business. Getting in the money is the smallest factor in the problem. Spending the results obtained by frantic appeals without inflicting actual harm on the next generation is a matter of the greatest difficulty, and has not hitherto, as a rule, been undertaken by persons of a calibre comparable with that possessed by those who succeed in business or professional life. The principal qualification of a charitable functionary is often held to be the adroitness with which he relieves the public of its cash, rather than the skill and success with which the cash is expended. Such functionaries are sometimes remunerated in part by receiving a commission on the money they succeed in obtaining from the public; a policy which taints charity with the sordidness of commerce without imparting the shrewdness and ability characteristic of the trading-classes.

Pestered, tormented, and badgered by the practised wiles of paid philanthropists, the charitable public are beginning to perceive that the subtle aroma of charity itself is prone to disappear before arriving at its destination. Impatience with the present system is on the increase. People who would give generously, if they were sure that their bounty would be effectual in doing good, refrain from giving because their taste and intellect revolt against the vulgarity of the appeals with which their support is demanded.

Personal contact between the giver and the object of his compassion is the only effectual method of replacing the system of charity by cheque—which is often no charity at all—at all events, to posterity. People sometimes dissipate their charities by giving a guinea here and a guinea there, when the concentration of a year's benevolence on one object might remedy an evil otherwise permanent and prolific. Sorrow and misery in the mass are essentially subjects for intellectual and practical, and not for emotional treatment. The sorrow or misery of a friend, on the other hand, is the subject for personal and sympathetic sacrifice. Much of the muddle into which charitable administration has fallen is the result of confusing two opposite ideas.

As the command of a ship or a regiment cannot be carried on by love and emotion, so the disciplined administration of charity in the mass can only be conducted successfully by rigid adherence to the fundamental principles of inexorable law. Neglect of such principles as the inviolable sanctity of parental responsibility; the justice of permitting free play to the natural consequences of criminal indolence; the effect on an innocent posterity of the fecundity of the unfit; and the essential differences between the province of natural law and the province of charity or gospel—has plunged the community into a slough of despair, under which the enormous sums annually provided for charitable purposes are not only making no inroad on the troubles of our race, but are instrumental to their perpetuation, by the subordination of generous, but untutored, emotions to the interests of a paid and blundering philanthropy.

Note.

Subjoined is the approximate income of the 1,013 metropolitan charities, contained in Mr. W. F. Howes' classified directory. This work seems to be carefully prepared, and to under, rather than to overstate the figures cited.

Approximate Income for 1883-4.

		£	s.	d.	£	s.	d.
4	Bible Societies	210,245	0	0			
14	Book and Tract Societies	78,736	0	0			
					288,981	0	0
57	Home Missions	521,678	0	0			
13	Home and Foreign Missions	248,495	0	0			
22	Foreign Missions	802,426	0	0			
					1,572,599	0	0
6	Church and Chapel Building Funds				31,483	0	0
26	Charities for the Blind	45,105	0	0			
8	Charities for Deaf and Dumb	14,388	0	0			
9	Charities for Incurables	44,958	0	0			
3	Charities for Idiots	56,000	0	0			
					160,451	0	0
	Carried forward				2,053,514	0	0

		£	s.	d.	£	s.	d.
	Brought forward				2,053,514	0	0
17	General Hospitals	341,896	0	0			
8	Consumption Hospitals	52,753	0	0			
5	Ophthalmic Hospitals	9,709	0	0			
3	Orthopedic Hospitals	5,150	0	0			
4	Skin Hospitals	4,714	0	0			
20	Hospitals for Women and Children	64,410	0	0			
5	Lying-in Hospitals	10,128	0	0			
28	Miscellaneous Special Hospitals	112,673	0	0			
					601,433	0	0
33	General Dispensaries	23,982	0	0			
13	Provident Dispensaries	10,310	0	0			
2	Institutions for Vaccination	2,662	0	0			
5	Do. for Surgical Appliances	12,384	0	0			
44	Convalescent Institutions	42,868	0	0			
14	Nursing Institutions	3,030	0	0			
					95,236	0	0
158	Pensions and Institutions for the Aged				435,710	0	0
95	Institutions for General Relief	312,010	0	0			
17	Food Institutions, Loan Charities, &c.	11,011	0	0			
					323,021	0	0
95	Voluntary Homes				127,506	0	0
55	Orphanages, &c.				150,941	0	0
73	Institutions for Reformation and Prevention				75,687	0	0
98	,, Education				444,083	0	0
42	,, Social Improvement				72,955	0	0
17	,, Protection				67,350	0	0
1,013	Grand Totals				£4,447,436	0	0

Conclusion.

Upon the dark foundations of our human nature shines the mysterous light of natural law. Welded together, on a supernatural forge, the correlation between the various phenomena of our social life is so firmly established as to render the separate cure of isolated symptoms beyond the range of the possible. The law governing correlation of social forces has not been formulated. But there is no ground for belief that universal law does not except from its dominion the phenomena displayed in the social life of man; or that isolated campaigns against objective evil are not productive of results both remoter and more important than are dreamed of in the philosophy of those who wage a guerilla warfare against them. Could we but see painted on the wall a connected panorama of the effects on future generations produced by the remedies commonly administered from the pharmacy of civilization, we should leap with horror from the folly and the wrong we now commit with gladness and singleness of heart.

Statesmen, administrators, philanthropists, who live and labour for this generation and for the present year, mobilise an invincible array of enemies against the innocent unborn. In tropic countries, during the season of drought, certain forms of insect and fish life totally disappear from the land, and become apparently as extinct as the apteryx of Mauritius, or the Moa of New Zealand. When the first warm rains of the monsoon awakens the sleeping energies of mother earth, the microscopic eggs of insects and the tiny spawn of fishes and of leeches, lurking invisible and unsuspected in the sandy bottoms of evaporated lakes while the earth is iron and the sky is brass, leap into a lusty and a vigorous life, when the falling rain supplies the environment needful for their activity and for their perfection. Not otherwise is it with the impregnable fecundity of philanthropic and legislative ova. The unfit are propagated, and posterity plagued if we ignore the stern conditions of natural law, which, so far as experience and research can guide us, are inexorable, continuous, and universal in their scope. Kindness by society to the individual is, as often as not, cruelty to potential individuals separated from us only by time, but who are as worthy to receive some of the enthusiasm of humanity as a fractional number of contemporary lives. Well it had been for us had our ancestors in some measure bethought themselves of the welfare of this generation, and had studied the consequences both of their neglect and of their primitive and emotional methods of beneficence. Had they surveyed from the higher standpoint of trustees for an improving race the methods of stamping out heredity of evil, and of extending to man himself the consideration that has long been given to improving the strain of dogs and the breed of horses, the task of solving the Problems of a Great City would neither be so dark nor so difficult as it now is. Like the lilies of the field, we, the ruling and imperial race among the nations of the earth, survive by dint of a blundering and irregulated vitality, rather than by taking thought for the morrow. And the measure we have meted out to ourselves we have dealt unto others.

The production of the great tragedy that is shaping itself on the plains of India and in the valleys of the Ganges and the Indus (as the consequence of English rule), cannot long be postponed. The materials of a similar tragedy are preparing wherever the hoof of a godless and hypocritical civilization has trodden underfoot the operation of natural law. Under the reign of the Moguls periodic famines so regulated the population of Hindostan as to adjust the numbers of the people to the capacity of the soil for maintaining them. When, more than a century since, English rule was first generally established throughout the Indian Peninsula, an equilibrium between the numbers of the people and the normal food supply was roughly but firmly established. In good years the population increased. In bad years the numbers of the people diminished. Those who survived numbered in the year 1800 about two hundred million souls. From that time to this, human life has been fostered and maintained at the sacrifice of all that makes life worth living. Internecine wars have been replaced by a universal passion for litigation between individuals. Famines have been minimised by Mansion House funds and by State aid, with such effect that the two hundred millions have been replaced by two hundred and fifty-seven millions of human beings. Those who would have died under the rougher and healthier rule of the Moguls, survive to a joyless and prolific existence. The pressure of population on the means of subsistence has destroyed the village arts that flourished for centuries before the baleful introduction of a sickly humanitarianism. Population and pressure increase after every famine, under the operation of law governing the abnormal fecundity of the unfit. Half-starved ryots survive the periodic death only to provide constituencies for future famines, of larger—and eventually, under present scientific and economic conditions—of unmanageable dimensions.

What is the humanity that feeds thousands, when the millions produced by feeding them must necessarily die a starving death of hopeless and unassuageable agony? When the next great Indian famine arrives, accompanied by abnormal modifications of the photosphere of the sun, dim suggestions will be offered as to the fatuity of attempting to confront the evidence of astronomical phenomena by the collection of a Mansion House fund.

The inference from such facts as these is, that we should attempt to harmonize our legislation and our public charities with the inexorable tendencies of natural law, that every member of society is irrevocably responsible for his or her contribution to the solution of the Problems of a Great City (which are the problems of the race), and cannot delegate them either to governments or to a clerical caste; and that the application of compassion alone, without the telescope of thought and judgment for those we have not seen, is to sow the dark seeds of poisonous and eternal evil.

When each of us admits the unsupportable burden of participation in the pollution and misery to which our wills have never consented, Œdipus has been found to answer the riddle propounded by the spirit of civilization. If each one answers *Davus sum non Œdipus*, the mysterious monster will continue to levy her tribute of human lives from the Bæotia of civilization. As every soul leaving England for a foreign country is involuntarily a missionary from his countrymen, a representative of their habits, aspirations, and enjoyments—and as by him, his character, and his conduct will native races keenly assess the value and estimate the nature of the civilization and religion he represents—so in a complex form of Society, such as that of a great city, is each soul forming part of it trustee for the race and the destinies of the race. The lightest act, imponderable as gossamer, is the parent of boundless and eternal issues. The slightest impulse and the lightest words are fraught alike with the qualities of eternal destiny. The period of incubation may be prolonged, but the germs are never sterile. Life or death, alike unseen and unrestricted, may be the inseparable consequences of the tiniest action. Europe condemned M. Ollivier for entering on war with a light heart. As men and women reach maturity each is told off in a contest between the powers of evil and of pain, and the powers of life and of light. We do not know with assurance the nature of the penalties following the betrayal of the trust reposed in us; but we do know the degradation and the corruption of national life that have resulted from the hollow profession of a perfect life, and from entering the terrible contest with a "light heart."

They are the most effectually solving the Problems of a Great City who by life and example add wisdom to the sacrifice of self. The tinkling cymbal of emotional and subsidized religion produces no large and permanent results on the lives and characters of the English people plunged in the sadness of a great city. Moral revolution in the individual is a panacea that cannot be replaced by legislation, nor by sermons, nor by alms. Such a revolution must begin among the comfortable classes, who alone enjoy the environment in which a moral change is generally possible, and the aim of the New revolution is the recognition by the comfortable classes of the fact that "pure religion and undefiled is to visit the fatherless and the widow in their affliction, and to keep himself unspotted from the world."

INDEX.

A.

Action of American Government, 66.
Adulteration, 154.
,,   Act of 1872, 155.
,,   Act of 1875, 156.
,,   of Beer, 158.
,,   of Bread, 156.
,,   of Butter, 159.
,,   Cag Mag Butchers, 160.
,,   of Cayenne, 158.
,,   of Cinnamon, 158.
,,   Code Napoléon, 161.
,,   of Curry Powder, 158.
,,   of Ginger, 158.
,,   of Honey, 158.
,,   of Isinglass, 157.
,,   of Mustard, 157.
,,   of Milk, 159.
,,   of Meat, 160.
,,   no remedy for, 162.
,,   of Pepper, 158.
,,   of Pickles, 160.
,,   Prussian Penal Code, 161.
,,   Sale of Foods Act, 155.
,,   of Spices, 158.
,,   of Spirits, 159.
,,   of Sugar, 159.
,,   of Tea, 156.
,,   Three flies, story of, 161.
,,   of Wines, 159.
Advertisement in *Times*, 51.

INDEX.

Agents-General, the, 74.
Amatonga Nation, 1, 48.
Anglo-Saxon Colonies, Governments of, 118.
Artizans Dwellings Act, 1882, 133.
  „   „   Improvements Acts, 1875, 1879, 1882, 133.
Australia, 66, 81.

B.

Bacon's Apothegm, 85.
Bank Holidays, 47.
Basuto Nation, 1, 48.
Bechuanaland, 86.
Besant, Mrs., 58.
Better dwellings for artizans and labourers, 132.
Bradlaugh, Mr., 58.
Booth, General, 8.

C.

Canada, 79.
Capital, serfs of, 154.
Cape Colony, 75, 80, 118.
Cawoods, the, 87.
Charities, 245.
  „   Approximate Income of, 257.
  „   Blind, twenty-six for the, 247.
  „   Defects of present system of, 246.
  „   Hospitals, enumeration of, 248.
  „   London, subscriptions to ninety-two hospitals in, 249.
  „   Metropolitan, revenue of, 245.
  „   Miscellaneous hospitals (twenty-nine), expenditure on, 248.
  „   Question of federation between, 249.
  „   Revenue, administration of, 253.
  „   Semi-fraudulent institutions, 250.
  „   Society for the Organization of Charitable Relief, 251.
Chinese Exclusion Acts, 142.
Code Napoléon, 33, 161.
Collier's Rents, 31.
Collision between classes, the, 18.
Colonial repugnance to receive Emigrants, 68.
  „   dependencies, business with England, 113.

Colonization, 116.
, , definition of, 116.
, , failures and schemes of, 122.
, , first principle guiding new settlement in, 127.
, , scheme, conditions of emigration under a, 123.
, , settlement, conditions and work involved in forming a, 119.
, , spots available for, 117.
Common Lodging Houses Act, 1851, 132.
Conclusion, the, 259.
, , India, coming tragedy in, 262.
, , India, famines in, 262.
, , Insect and fish life, certain forms of, 262.
Criminal and pauperized classes, 48.
Criminals, segregation of, 50.

D.

Destination of emigrants, 89.
Democracy in Anglo-Saxon Colonies, 74.
Division of the evil, 25.
Doubleday, 31.
Drink, the, 165.
, , Alabama Claims, 168.
, , Bismarck, Prince, 165.
, , Interests, the, 168.
, , East End, Palace of Delight in, 173.
, , East End, in the, 174.
, , Gothenburg system, main features of, 176.
, , Läger beer, 168.
, , remedy for, 167.
, , Rivals to public-house, 170.
, , Shaftesbury estate, the, 169.
, , St. Boniface to Archbishop of Canterbury, 175.
, , Temperance movement, the, 166.

E.

England, average death-rate in, 131.
, , rubbish heap, a, 144.
, , untaxed strangers in, 144.
English cant, 48.

Emigrants, protector of, 149.
Emigration, 64.
," England's practice with regard to, 110.
," Societies, 72.
," Bureau, 77, 79.
," funds for, 83.

F.

Federation, 113.
Female labour, 18.
Forms of faith, 7.

G.

Gautama, beatitudes of, 2.
Germany, 93.
," attitude of, towards emigration, 96.
," emigration from, to British N. America and Australia, 97.
," emigration in 1884, 99.
," "Börsen Halle," extract from, 99.
," emigration, letter on, 100.
," emigration, loss through, 97.
," military system in, 98, 100.
," population of, 97.
Germans, number of, in London, 96.
Grosvenor Square, 31.

H.

Himalayan tribes, 1.
Hungary, 106.
," causes of emigration from, 107.
," Measures against emigration agencies, 107.
," population of, 109.
Hypocrisy, 14.

I.

Increase of population, 32, 71.
Information Bureau, 114.
Information as to industrial conditions ruling in Great Britain, 78.
Institutions for general relief, expenditure on, 83.

J.

Jewish community, 53.
Jews, emigration of, 141.

L.

Law, 25.
Labouring classes, Lodging Houses Act, 1851, 132.
Limitation of families, 58.
London, dock gates at, 11.
,,   distress in, 226.
,,   foreigners in, 143.
,,   government of, 227.
,,   municipality for, 153.
,,   nomads, 14.
,,   unemployed, 67.
,,   water supply of, 136.

M.

Mahomet, exhortation of, 154.
Malthusians, the, 16.
Manning, Cardinal, 53.
Mansion House Committee, 59.
Marriage, 33.
Marriages at Fifteen, 44.
Medical Science, 28.
Mortuaries, absence of general system of, 138.
Metropolitan and District Railways, extension of, 146.

N.

National Debt, 13.
,,   Association for Promoting State Directed Colonization, 69.
,,   Emigration Council, 90.
National scheme of emigration, advantages of, 115.
New South Wales, 75.
New Zealand, 76.
Norway, 102.
,,   attitude of towards emigration, 105.
,,   emigration from, during years 1880-4, 104.
,,   Gothenburg system in, 106
,,   population of, 104.

Norway, principal causes of emigration from, 102.
Notes to Chapter III., 61.
Nuisances, Removal Act, 1885, 132.
    ,,   Inspectors of, 149.

O.

Offensive trades, 137.
Overcrowding, 130.
    ,,   demolitions serious factor in, 147.
    ,,   partly due to, 139.

P.

Passengers Act, 111.
    ,,   ,,   amendment of, 112.
Paupers, 12.
Pawnbrokers Act, the, 221.
Peabody, George, 65.
Peter the Hermit, 40.
Philanthropy, 24.
Pitakas, three books of, 2.
Poor Laws, the, 226.
Poor Man's Budget, the, 208.
    ,, ,, Scaffolder, beer consumption of, 211.
    ,, ,, ,, boots for family of, 220.
    ,, ,, ,, butchers' meat for family of, 217.
    ,, ,, ,, budget expenditure of, 220.
    ,, ,, ,, coals for, 218.
    ,, ,, ,, clothes for family of, 219.
    ,, ,, ,, co-operation for, 221.
    ,, ,, ,, dinner of, 218.
    ,, ,, ,, direct and indirect taxes paid by, 221.
    ,, ,, ,, expenditure in drink of, 208, 212.
    ,, ,, ,, expenditure in tobacco of, 209, 213.
    ,, ,, ,, family, maintenance of, 218.
    ,, ,, ,, pawnshop, use of to, 221.
    ,, ,, ,, rent of, 213, 214, 217.
    ,, ,, ,, rent of, letter in connection with, 215.
    ,, ,, ,, wages of, 208.
Poor, inability of to protect themselves, 149.
Public Prosecutor, the, 152.

R.

Religion, 9.
Red Church, the (of Bethnal Green), 36.
Rent, 140.
„ and wages, disproportion between, 140.
Returns of questions put to 50 men employed by sweating tailors and remarks appended thereto, 18.
Roman Catholic Church, the, 32, 52.
Royal Commission on the Housing of the Working Classes (1885), 132.

S.

Sermon on the Mount, the, 1.
Sterilization of Unfit, 60.
Singer, Rev. S., 54.
St. Luke's, ophthalmia in, 131.
St. Pancras, death-rate in, 131.
Socialism, 179.
„ "Are you a Social Democrat?" 199.
„ Baron Rothschild, imprisonment of, 179.
„ Bright, Mr., 193.
„ Comfortable classes, selfishness of, 193.
„ Competition, 195.
„ Champion, Mr. H. H., views on, 184.
„ Criminals under, 204.
„ Employers' Liability Act, the, 198.
„ English strides in, 179.
„ Equality of personality under, 194.
„ Factory Acts, the, 196.
„ House owners liable for insanitary condition of premises, 197.
„ Idleness, punishment of, 204.
„ Kropotkine, 202.
„ London, Local Government of, 201.
„ Moral wrong, cause of evil, 189.
„ no future State according to, 181.
„ Professor Fawcett on programme of, 182.
„ Robinson Crusoe, case of, 190.
„ Social Democratic Party, the, 180.
„ Science, 202.

W

Socialism, State, interference of the, 196.
," State help, 206.
," Statute Book, fragmentary acceptances of a principle in, 196.
," "The Times" on, 188.
," Ten Commandments, the, 193.
," Two evils, choice between, 192.
," ultimate purposes of, 184.
," Workers, the, 198.
," Working man, right interest in, 193.
South Africa, 66, 85.
Strong, the, overwhelmed by unfit, 30.

U.

Unemployed, the, 223.
," Agricultural labourers among the, 237.
," Artizans (skilled) among the, 236.
," East End parishes and rates, 239.
," Fecundity of, 225.
," Government, responsibilty of, to, 240.
," house in West End open to, 232.
," London, creation of defences for, by, 243.
," London, distress in, 226.
," London, government of, 227.
," Mansion House funds effect on, 224.
," materials of army of, 229-233.
," measures to solve the problem appertaining to the, 243.
," Poor Laws, the, 226.
," relief works for, 241.
," Soldiers, 233.
," Soldier, suicide of, 235.
," Workhouse labour test for, 238.
United States, the, 66.

V.

Vestries and Boards of Guardians, gross neglect of, 133.
," ," ," law on the duties of, 134.
Vestrymen and Local Government, 151.

INDEX.

Village Council, a, 121.
Virginia, first English colony planted in, 128.

W.

Waterlow, Sir Sydney, 65.
Woman of New York, a, 50.

Z.

Zulu Nation, the, 1, 48.

www.ingramcontent.com/pod-product-compliance
Lightning Source LLC
Chambersburg PA
CBHW031342230426
43670CB00006B/418